CARRIE MAE WEEMS

The Hampton Project

Carrie M. Weems

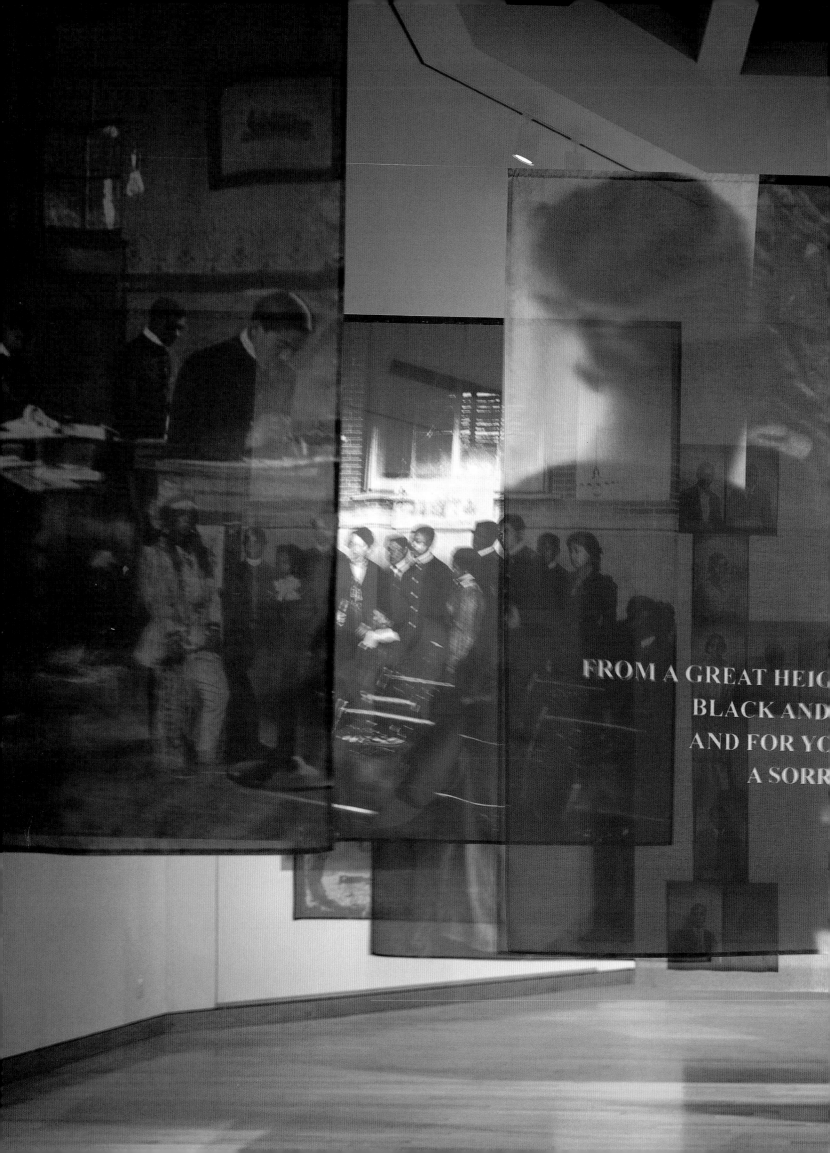

FROM A GREAT HEIG
BLACK AND
AND FOR YC
A SORR

The photographs on the previous pages and all full-page photographs hereafter
are installation images and banners from *Carrie Mae Weems: The Hampton Project*, 2000,
a series of digital photographs printed on muslin and canvas in variable dimensions, as installed at
the Williams College Museum of Art, Williamstown, Massachusetts, March 4–October 22, 2000.

An audiotaped text by Carrie Mae Weems entitled *Before and After*, which accompanies *The Hampton Project*,
appears in its entirety with the banners and installation views throughout the book.

CARRIE MAE WEEMS

The Hampton Project

By Vivian Patterson

With Essays by

Frederick Rudolph / Constance W. Glenn /

Deborah Willis-Kennedy / Jeanne Zeidler

Interview by Denise Ramzy and Katherine Fogg

APERTURE

IN ASSOCIATION WITH WILLIAMS COLLEGE MUSEUM OF ART,

WILLIAMSTOWN, MASSACHUSETTS

ONE HUNDRED YEARS OF DIFFERENCE

I remain amazed at how exhibition concepts can develop.
In October 1995, I was invited to a dinner by the
Williamstown Art Conservation Center bringing together
the participants in the groundbreaking conservation project
and exhibition *To Conserve a Legacy: American Art from
Historically Black Colleges and Universities.* After perusing
the guest list, I realized Hampton University Museum
would be represented. I remembered from many years
earlier a remarkable catalog
for an exhibition of pho-
tographs called *The Hampton
Album*, and wondered what
the connection was. In 1966
the Museum of Modern Art
in New York had published a
catalog documenting their
collection of Frances
Benjamin Johnston's 1900
photographs of the Hampton
Normal and Agricultural
Institute; the work had been
acquired by Lincoln Kirstein,
who also wrote the catalog.
With some satisfaction, I was
able to put my hands on the
actual publication in my
bookcase; I had bought it
nearly thirty years earlier. Other than the beautiful
photographs that had stayed in my memory, I knew little
about the Hampton Normal and Agricultural Institute.
Imagine my surprise when I learned that the founder of the
school in Hampton, Virginia, was Samuel Chapman
Armstrong, an 1862 graduate of Williams College! At
dinner I met Mary Lou Hultgren, the museum's curator,
who was completely knowledgeable about General
Armstrong and the relationship between Williams and
Hampton. This relationship, mediated by Johnston's
compelling images, hinted at the possibility of a future
exhibition celebrating this connection.

Frances Benjamin Johnston (American, 1864–1952),

Self-portrait, date unknown

We felt that a contemporary artist's perspective
on the past as portrayed by Johnston would provide a
counterpoint, and even tension, which could make for an
unforgettable encounter between two artists spanning one
hundred years. Carrie Mae Weems immediately came to
mind as the perfect person to handle such a broad and
open-ended assignment.

Indeed, *Carrie Mae Weems: The Hampton Project* would
appear to be an ideal under-
taking for the Williams
College Museum of Art. It
was conceived as a two-part
exhibition that would bring
together the haunting photographs of nineteenth-
century photographer Frances
Benjamin Johnston and a
newly commissioned work
by contemporary African
American photographer
Carrie Mae Weems. The
subject for both would be
the Hampton Normal and
Agricultural Institute.
For a teaching museum
dedicated to involving as
many academic departments
as possible in the study of art, we marveled at the
possibilities that such a venture could offer simultaneously
for American studies and history, African American studies,
women's studies, the history and practice of photography,
as well as alumni across the country. We were most
fortunate that important funding sources agreed with our
assessment of the richness and potential of such an effort.
First and foremost, I want to thank the National Endowment for the Arts for their initial grant that gave us the
impetus to proceed. Their support encouraged us to
vigorously pursue the project and secure further funding.
Grants from the John S. and James L. Knight Foundation,

the Rockefeller Foundation, and the Peter Norton Family Foundation enabled us to realize the exhibition and publication with the level of excellence and professionalism an institution always hopes to achieve. Additional support came from Clay and Garrett Kirk, Williams College class of 1963, for which we are very grateful.

All exhibition projects are complicated, but reconciling changes that have taken place over the course of a century is daunting; *Carrie Mae Weems: The Hampton Project* is no exception. An artist's interpretation of historical material, or any material for that matter, should be presented openly and without apology, but we all know that one person's freedom can be another's tyranny, and that we all see the world differently. Moreover, there is always risk involved in commissioning a new work by any artist. Frances Benjamin Johnston (1864–1952) was commissioned in 1899 to photograph the Hampton Normal and Agricultural Institute for display at the 1900 Paris Exposition. Carrie Mae Weems was commissioned to revisit the Johnston photographs and life at Hampton University. In other words, she was able to define the parameters of her commission.

Carrie Mae Weems, detail of *Untitled* (Woman standing alone), from "Untitled (Kitchen Table Series)," 1990

The artist and photographer Carrie Mae Weems has distinguished herself for her narrative explorations of self and identity. This project provided her with the opportunity to examine the complex role of race and education over the past one hundred years at one of the most renowned historically black universities. Hampton University is unique in that Native American students are also an integral part of its history. During her visits to Hampton, Carrie was given full access to Hampton's extraordinarily rich photographic archives, which consist not only of Johnston's acclaimed *Album*, but also contain a diverse body of photographic and historical material documenting life at Hampton since its beginnings. I am very grateful for the museum and university's generosity in graciously sharing the wealth of the archives for this project.

Many individuals and institutions have been involved in the successful realization of this effort. I would like to thank our associate curator, Vivian Patterson, for her dedicated pursuit of excellence and her oversight of a project that called for a command of post–Civil War culture in the South, photography both historical and contemporary, women's studies, the history of education in this country, U.S. Indian policy, not to mention Williams College history and Carrie Mae Weems. As the curator who oversees the museum's permanent collection, Vivian is used to unusual and seemingly unrelated groupings, but this project required extraordinary resources on her part. The major components to the project are the exhibition; its national tour; the symposium, which took place in April 2000; and this publication. Vivian's commitment to presenting the work of Weems and Johnston in the galleries, both in Williamstown and across the country, in print, and as the subject of a daylong symposium, has been notable, and I am deeply appreciative of her efforts.

Carrie Mae Weems's involvement has been both inspiring and energizing. We are most grateful to her for her remarkable installation and her collaboration with us on all aspects of this project. On her behalf, I would also like to acknowledge the Dean's Office of Williams College; through its auspices, Carrie was able to teach and be a powerful presence on campus during the spring 2000 semester as the prestigious Sterling A. Brown, Class of 1922, Visiting Professor.

Associate Director Marion Goethals must be warmly thanked for her administrative, editorial, and moral guidance throughout this process. During my absences she oversaw countless aspects of the project with her characteristic calm and wisdom; I cannot begin to thank her sufficiently. As always, our preparation crew, directed by Hideyo Okamura, with the assistance of Pat Holden and Greg Smith, performed their challenging task of installing the exhibition with imagination and skill. Also crucial to the success of the exhibition have been Toddy and Doug Munson of Chicago Albumen Works in Housatonic, Massachusetts, and Curator Peter Galassi and Associate Curator M. Darsie Alexander of the Photography Department of the Museum of Modern Art. They provided the photographs by Frances B. Johnston, the former with their modern platinum prints taken from originals belonging to the Hampton University Museum, and the latter with their generous loan of six vintage images.

The museum's annual *Prendergast Symposium: Studies in American Art*, funded each year by the Eugénie Prendergast Trust, was an unforgettable event this year. Divided into two sessions—Race and Education, and Race and Visual Representation—the day was electric with creativity, scholarship, new information, and extraordinary camaraderie. I would like to thank the participants: Robert Engs, associate professor of history, University of Pennsylvania; Jeffrey L. Hamley, dean of the Center for Arts and Cultural Studies, Institute of American Indian Arts in Santa Fe; E. Barry Gaither, director of the Museum of the National Center of Afro-American Artists, Inc., Boston; artists Nayland Blake, Tim Rollins, and James Luna; Deborah Willis-Kennedy, Director of Exhibitions, Anacostia Museum and Center for African American History and Culture, Smithsonian Institution; Williams College Assistant Professor of Political Science Mark T. Reinhardt; and especially Carrie Mae Weems, for her flawless keynote address/performance, which was aided so beautifully by artist and musician Terry Adkins.

We are delighted this publication has been designed and published by Aperture Foundation, noted for their elegant and substantive books on photography. Editor Phyllis Thompson Reid and designer Michelle Dunn Marsh demonstrated infectious enthusiasm, knowledge, and talent with their work on this volume. While it is intended to function as documentation of the show, it is also a book in its own right, with a focus on the fabric works of Carrie Mae Weems, particularly *The Hampton Project*, and with a formidable array of essays by Frederick Rudolph, Mark Hopkins Professor of History, Emeritus, Williams College; Constance W. Glenn, director, University Art Museum at California State University, Long Beach; Deborah Willis-Kennedy, Jeanne Zeidler, director of the Hampton University Museum; and of course, Vivian Patterson. To each of them, I extend my heartfelt thanks. Students Katherine Fogg and Denise Ramzy, both of whom graduated this June, demonstrated unwavering interest in and enthusiasm for the unique opportunity to work with Carrie Mae Weems during her residency. The resulting interview has proven to be invaluable to our understanding of the artist and how she works. Photographer Arthur Evans admirably met the difficult challenge of photographing Weems's three fabric suites—*Ritual & Revolution, The Jefferson Suites,* and *The Hampton Project*—with the evocative yet lucid results reproduced here. It has been a pleasure and an honor to join forces again with Susan Dillmann, our former public relations coordinator, who took on the role of editorial consultant for this book; she proved true to memory in her impeccable professionalism and remarkable ability.

As is often the case, the focus for the project evolved over time. I have always believed that working with contemporary artists involves a leap of faith; once an artist is selected, the process inevitably becomes collaborative. And this time other parties, Hampton University and the Hampton University Museum, also contributed significantly to the effort. Originally intended to travel to Hampton, the show will not be presented there because of differences of opinion about the way historical materials are used. I very much respect Hampton museum director Jeanne Zeidler's decision. While I had anticipated a meeting of the minds between Johnston and Weems, I had not expected such a vivid display of these "hundred years of difference." It is my hope that we can all benefit from a better understanding of our histories and stories, realizing that differences always develop when least expected.

—LINDA SHEARER
Director, Williams College Museum of Art

ALLA MEMORIA
DI OTTAVIANO BARDOLI MOSSITE
NATO NOVARA IL XXII APRILE MDCCXVI
E MORTO IN PISA IL XI MARZO MDCCLXXXIX
IL FRATEL PONSE LA PATRIA

LA SCIENZA E GLI PROFESSITA
NE ATTESTA I MERITI EMINENTI
E LA PERENNITÀ DELLA GLORIA
ARTEFICE DEL MONUMENTO
FU GIOVANNI DUPRÈ

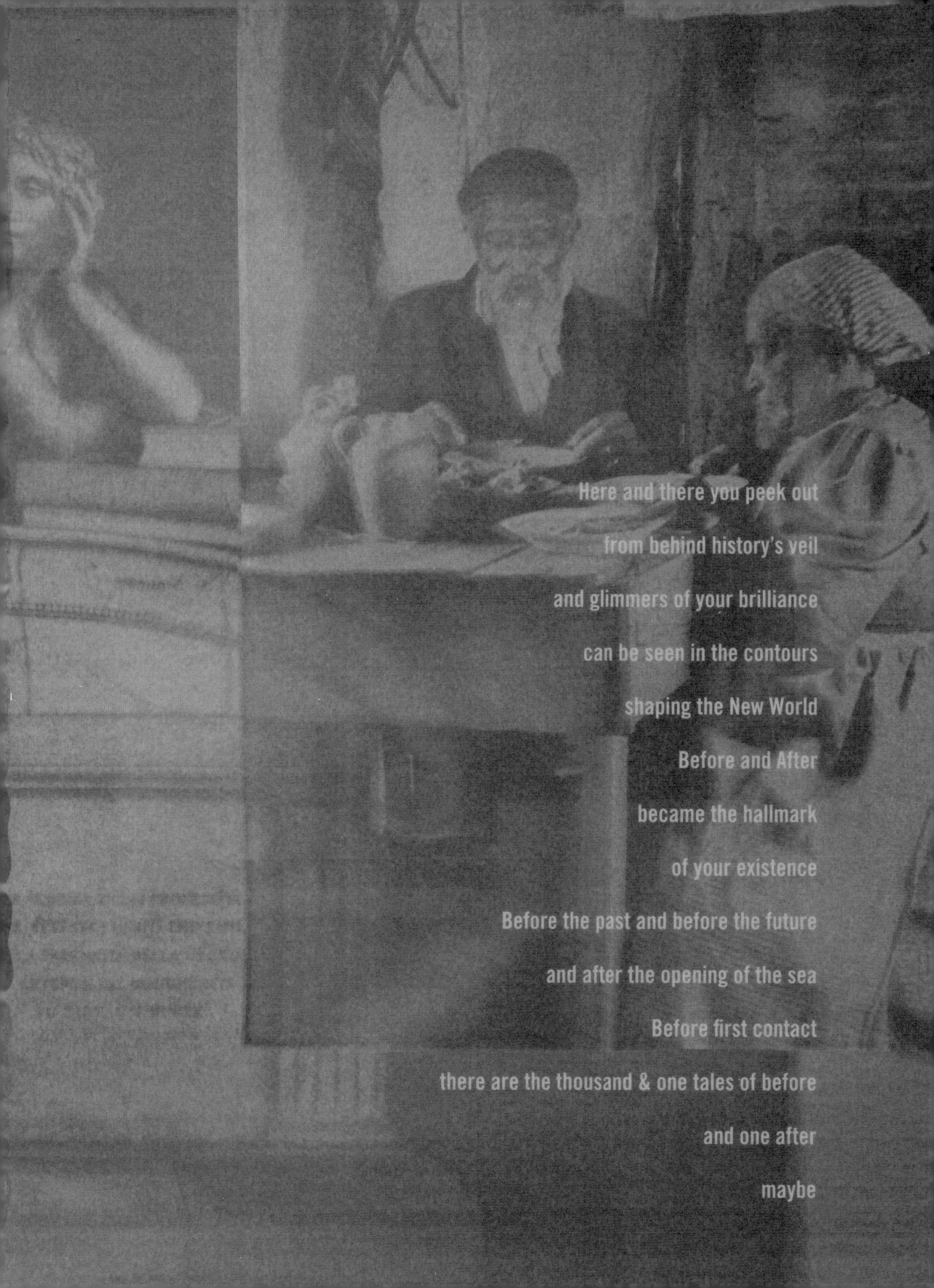

Here and there you peek out

from behind history's veil

and glimmers of your brilliance

can be seen in the contours

shaping the New World

Before and After

became the hallmark

of your existence

Before the past and before the future

and after the opening of the sea

Before first contact

there are the thousand & one tales of before

and one after

maybe

Here and there you peek out

from behind history's veil

and glimmers of your brilliance

can be seen in the contours

shaping the New World

Before and After

became the hallmark

of your existence

Before the past and before the future

and after the opening of the sea

Before first contact

there are the thousand & one tales of before

and one after

maybe

THE HAMPTON PROJECT

Material concerns preoccupy Carrie Mae Weems as she continues to expand the perspectives of her work and artistry. Over the course of her career as an image-maker, she has nurtured her creative talents and honed her critical eye. She has widened her focus from the personal and the political to deal with larger societal issues of color, gender, identity, and class. Now she marshals her con-siderable abilities to mine rich cultural themes, striving for the portrayal of universal narratives that offer insight into national and world histories and, ultimately, into the human condition.

Weems herself states: "My responsibility as an artist is to work, to sing for my supper, to make art, beautiful and powerful, that adds and reveals; to beautify the mess of a messy world, to heal the sick and feed the helpless; to shout bravely from the roof-tops and storm barricaded doors and voice the specifics of our historic moment." [1]

Hand in hand with this passionate embrace of collective themes is Weems's sustained effort to extend the parameters of her art practice and to emancipate her artistic means—her chosen medium of photography—to serve the myriad purposes of her message. As she produces work that addresses her predetermined issues, she reaches for complementary methods of communication that assure a dimensional encounter and accentuate the reflexivity of her art and her audience.

This said, it is certainly no surprise that Weems has added a variety of ingredients to her recipe for visual success. She has incorporated words, captions, and catch phrases, whether imbedded in her imagery or in accompanying printed and displayed texts; she has added audiotaped commentaries, extended prose narratives, sound, and music to the body of several photographic essays; she has chosen to mingle wallpaper with suites of her pictures, as well as incorporate sculpture within her installations. She has also used materials normally beyond the purview of the photographer, familiar and mundane items from our daily lives, as viable canvases for her work.

Porcelain plates, a "welcome" mat, martini glasses, a record and its slip jacket—everyday objects have been transformed into mysterious signifiers and portentous monuments. Similarly, her use of fabric in her work is a natural extension of her manic drive "to make her (visual) expression truer to her own experience of the world as well as meaningful and accessible to a wider audience." [2]

Weems declares: "I want to make things that are beautiful, seductive, formally challenging and culturally meaningful. But somehow, I also imagine that, within the confines of the art world, I insert a voice that is somewhat different. It's a voice that assumes cultural fluidity. I'm also committed to radical social change—that's the reason that themes of social relations recur in my art practice. . . . Any form of human injustice moves me deeply . . . the battle against all forms of oppression keeps me going and keeps me focused." [3]

Weems charms and engages the viewer by employing established aesthetic forms that make traditional art beautiful. Then she insinuates her message into these alluring works; and that message, while always intellectual, can sometimes be aggressive or contentious. It is her inventiveness in merging the two that results in works that, though they exist initially as objects of contemplation and seduction, ultimately prevail as objects of provocation. She offers us pieces that seem to fit comfortably within the status quo, but that in the end prove to be irritants and catalysts challenging viewers to confront their own beliefs, prejudices, and values. Hers is enticement with intent to confound and often disturb.

Carrie Mae Weems's career, which she has built over the past two decades, is well documented, her artworks and message widely known. *The Hampton Project*, the artist's most recent commission (for the Williams College Museum of Art in Williamstown, Massachusetts), lives within that career and is part of a proclaimed trilogy of fabric suites—with *Ritual & Revolution* and *The Jefferson Suites*—produced during the period 1998–2000.

Carrie Mae Weems grew up in Oregon in the 1950s, the daughter of a sharecropper family from Mississippi. After high school, she journeyed to San Francisco to study modern dance, supporting herself with a progression of jobs in restaurants, offices, and factories, and becoming politically active in socialist organizations and the feminist movement. Though she was given a camera in the early 1970s, her use of it for creative purposes and her pursuit of photography as a professional artist occurred later. She received a B.F.A. from the California Institute of Arts, Valencia, in 1981 and an M.F.A. in photography from the University of California, San Diego, in 1984.

Weems's first major series of photographic work, and a precedent for "The Hampton Project," was "Family Pictures and Stories," produced over the period 1978–1984. A variant of "the family album," this intimate and caring piece combines images of her father and mother's families (the Weemses and Polks) with audio narratives of their migration from Mississippi to Oregon in the 1940s and 1950s and the artist's own first-person text commentary.[4]

Untitled (Man and mirror), from "Untitled (Kitchen Table Series)," 1990

The six–year process of creating "Family Pictures and Stories" prompted the artist to pursue the study of folklore in the Graduate Program in Folklore at the University of California, Berkeley, electing the oral traditions existing within African American culture and the storytelling customs of Africa as her area of concentration. For Weems, storytelling as an expression of and vehicle for interpretation was soon adopted as a hallmark of her art practice.[5]

Her efforts at this time were rooted in issues relating to race and representation, examining—and then detonating—pervasive images that reinforce the negative perception of African Americans. Subsequent work became more obviously political. Her series "Ain't Jokin' " (1987–1988), and its counterpart "American Icons" (1988–1989), manifest Weems's examination of lingering, insidious racism in all our lives and address American humor's perpetuation of racial stereotypes. For Weems, jokes are a social barometer and a communally sanctioned way to touch on topics that, in genteel conversation, would otherwise be considered unmentionable.

"Ain't Jokin' " proffers straightforward portraits of African Americans paired with racist jokes and catch phrases in an effort first to establish a dissonance, and then to provoke the viewer's sense of shock and shame upon recognition of his/her internal, subliminal prejudices. With the same disquieting results, "American Icons" focuses on fragments of material culture, kitsch, still life, and domestic interiors as signifiers of similar malignant racist opinion. "Colored People" (1989–1990) continues the artist's production of layered and psychologically complex work calculated to blindside the viewer.[6]

In 1987, while on a month-long fellowship at the Smithsonian Institution, Weems spent time researching African American cultural idioms, looking at those period images and representations of African Americans throughout the history of American photography held in the Institution's collections. She turned to some favorite things: Zora Neale Hurston's writings, jazz and the blues, and folk painting and drawing. From this, Weems produced "a tribute to the role of the stage in early expressions of African American culture"[7] that became manifest in her piece *Ode to Affirmative Action* (1989).

Also in 1990, Weems debuted "Untitled (Kitchen Table Series)," an introspective and poetically evocative work laced with the visual richness of a theater set. Twenty images and thirteen text panels, portrayals of a young woman (Weems herself) in the company of a few female friends and children, and the occasional male visitor, combine to create poignant, domestic vignettes. Beneath the stark glare of a single hanging light, the cast takes its place at the far end of a table; the viewer's seat is at the near end. We are braced for a narrative steeped in the personal; we feel Weems has set the stage for a *tableau vivant* starring African American individuals. However, she ultimately raises the curtain on a drama of societies and an opportunity for reflection on what is universal: everyman/ everywoman involved in everyday relationships, their emotional experiences, and the many subtle concerns human interaction entails. [8]

At first glance "Untitled (Kitchen Table Series)" seems to explore human experience from the vantage of a female subject and viewer, and it seems to have an emphatic African American point of view.

Detail from *Your Place or Mine's*, 1992

Nonetheless, the images also exist outside the realm of gender and race. Weems has commented that "one of the things I was thinking about was whether it might be possible to use black subjects to represent universal concerns." [9] Everson Museum Senior Curator Thomas Piché, in his essay in *Carrie Mae Weems: Recent Work, 1992–1998*, writes, "Weems has insisted on the black subject being treated as part of the fabric of the larger society. What affects blacks, affects all. What they affect has ramifications in other communities. She holds that her use of the black subject is not self-referential, that the black subject can speak for more than itself, that it can

speak across race and class lines to issues of isolated identity; to how we participate in the construction of our lives and are accomplices to our social situations; and to other concerns that affect all humankind." [10]

In 1991 Carrie Mae Weems created a fully active environment titled "And 22 Million Very Tired and Very Angry People." Mounted as an installation, large-scale framed Polaroid color prints were joined by fifteen white or red quote-laden banners—floating signifiers—hung from the gallery ceiling. Emblematic captions and texts were silk-screened onto the banners and individual picture mats to effect a consortium of voices addressing questions of inequality and advocating profound global social reform. It was her first series not to concentrate on photographic portraits and the first to speak forthrightly of those revolutionaries, theorists, and social activists who inform her work. [11]

Upon completing "Untitled (Kitchen Table Series)" and after "And 22 Million Very Tired and Very Angry People," Weems created "Commemorating" in 1992, an edition of twenty Lenox china dinner plates, ivory in color, ringed with gold, and with a text displayed in the center of each. Providing an alternative to the (racist) figurines that inhabited "American Icons," the tableware celebrates the achievements of African Americans and those who have assisted their cause. As Curator Dana Friis-Hansen points out, plates play a functional and quiet domestic role, yet these elegant objects reaffirm a marginalized history. [12]

Also in 1991 Weems was invited to participate in an Artist-in-Residence Program sponsored by The Fabric Workshop/Museum in Philadelphia, Pennsylvania. The collaborative projects that ensued over the next three years served to continue and consolidate her commitment to the union of image and text; but more importantly, she wholeheartedly embraced a medium until then used only peripherally in her work—fabric.

Veiled sentiments began to suffuse Weems's art as she became fluent in the medium she adopted as a part of her work at the Fabric Workshop/Museum. The highlight of Weems's residency in Philadelphia was the creation of a large folding screen titled *The Apple of Adam's Eye* (1993), a stunning piece combining a photograph of Weems, draped and veiled in deep blue, silk-screened onto orange-red cotton sateen, and a text embroidered in silk and gold thread. This multi-paneled work for the most part has been exhibited with photographs and texts from the artist's "Africa Series" produced the same year.

The text embroidered on the screen and those infusing Weems's "Africa Series" deal with the relationships between the first man and the first woman and basic, primal impulses: desire, love, pleasure, pain, temptation, sin, betrayal, and power. [13] On the front of the screen,

The Apple of Adam's Eye, 1993

framing the draped and veiled figure, is a text that reads, "She'd always been the apple/Of Adam's eye." On the reverse of the central panel, Weems has inscribed, "Temptation, my ass, desire has its place, and besides, they were both doomed from the start."

Why would Weems be so drawn to cloth? It is most likely due to the medium's limitless potential for communication. In their book *Cloth and the Human Experience* (1989), Annette B. Weiner and Jane Schneider propose that, on a world-wide scale, complex moral and ethical issues related to dominance and autonomy, opulence and poverty, political legitimacy and succession,

and gender and sexuality all find ready expression through cloth. Also manifest in fabric is how readily its appearance and its literal makeup evoke ideas of connectedness and binding. Indeed, cloth metaphors echo from all parts of the world, today as in the past. "Social scientists and laypersons regularly describe society as fabric, woven or knit together. Cloth as a metaphor for society, thread for social relations, express more than connectedness, however. The softness and ultimate fragility of these materials capture the vulnerability of humans, whose very relationship is transient…." [14]

Assuredly Weems thinks of fabric as a great connector, binding humans not only to each other, but also to ancestors and descendants—the past and the future. She appreciates cloth for its visual and rich tactile sense, as well as its malleability and capacity to reveal or conceal identities and values. In "And 22 Million Very Tired and Very Angry People," the artist focused on the conventional (and political) use of cloth as a vehicle for communication by tapping the propagandist tradition of banners. Aware of the history of political and religious groups' dependency on cloth (banners, flags, uniforms) to mobilize human emotions in support of specific causes, she deployed banners, peppered with quotes from such thinkers as Antonio Gramsci, Rosa Luxemburg, and Malcolm X, as accents to the overall scheme of her exhibit. Then, in 1998 and again in 1999, Weems created two comprehensive fabric environments, each of which subsumes the viewer in intellectual and emotional depths—*Ritual & Revolution* and *The Jefferson Suites*. The first two of an anticipated trilogy (ending with *The Hampton Project*), they share the same general formal dimensions: large diaphanous banners, hung floor to ceiling, bearing digitally reproduced

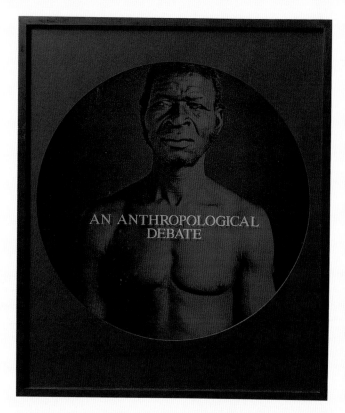
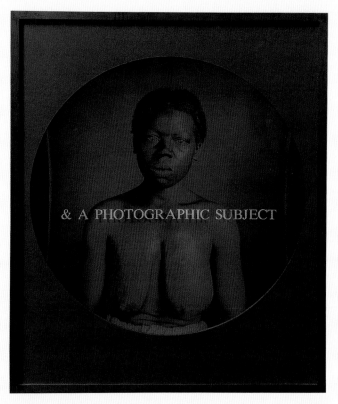

Above and above right: *An Anthropological Debate* and *& A Photographic Subject*, from "From Here I Saw What Happened and I Cried," 1995–96

images that are layered and clustered to accentuate the reflexivity of the images, in concert with text and audio proposing at once the voices of auteur, narrator, participant, and omniscient observer.

"*Ritual & Revolution* (1998) tells the story of human struggle, challenge, and loss. It is a lament and a testament to the endurance of mankind."[15] Upon its installation at the University of California at Berkeley Art Museum, Director Jacquelynn Baas wrote:

> Both a continuation and a broadening of Weems's past themes, Ritual & Revolution *intends to be a public forum for cultural dialogue as well as a private meditative experience. It integrates images of natural beauty and human achievement with references to cruelty, suffering, and revolution against oppression. The references are poetic, yet very specific; they range through history, from the Russian Revolution, to the Irish potato famine, and the Holocaust. The recitation of these specifics yields a cumulative awareness of human frailty and courage, and generates feelings of love for our be-knighted species.*[16]

Suspended from the ceiling in a wedge-shaped formation, twelve banners of variable dimension bear

ghostly images of the ruins of a Mayan courtyard at Tulum, Mexico; Puvier's Garden; a stairway at Versailles; ancient temple steps; the inhabited skyline of a southwestern Hopi community; an archaic Greek sculpture; and the slave coast viewed from a slave holding facility in Ghana. These mix to create "a global geography of ruin as a site for meditation."[17] They are joined by additional images of Holocaust victims, a Birmingham, Alabama, riot incident, and bound and blindfolded captives. As the viewer navigates around the banners, "the evanescent sheerness of the banners' thin muslin fabric enhances the fragility of the images . . . the visual shifts produce a layering effect, giving rise to palimpsest-like relationships between the individual images. In this way, *Ritual & Revolution* fulfills the aspiration of installation art to engage the entire body of the viewer in the production of meaning."[18]

The Jefferson Suites, which opened at the Santa Barbara Museum of Art in December 1999, takes on the topic of genetics. The title alludes to the DNA analysis of the descendants of Thomas Jefferson and his African American slave and mistress Sally Hemings that proved genetic fraternity. The seventeen semitransparent muslin banners,[19] ranging in size from approximately four-by-eight feet to eight-by-ten feet and accompanied by a thirteen-minute musical score interwoven with a Weems narrative, make manifest the artist's ideas and concerns regarding modern DNA technology. The banners are printed with images relating to biotechnology and cultural turning points in genetic science: Darwin and one of his thirteen finches (standing for diversity within a species); a scientist; the first test-tube baby; Timothy Wilson Spencer (the first person executed for a crime solved solely on DNA evidence); a gibbon monkey and a child at play (representing those two degrees of separation, the difference in the number of chromosomes between the two beings); Wall Street (denoting the profits to be garnered by DNA research); Dolly (the first cloned mammal); and the Capitol Building in Washington, D.C. (America's seat of legislative power and legal sanction for genetic exploration). These are joined by images of a chanteuse flanked by her band, the Busch String Quartet, and two "enactments": one of the Clinton-Lewinsky affair, the other of the Jefferson-Hemings association. Four additional photographs, each an image of a nude's back inscribed with one of the four chemical "letters" of the DNA alphabet—adenine, thymine, cytosine, and guanine—complete the suite with Duchampian flair. The ensuing argument that differences perennially sustained across races are now only skin deep and may be summarily dismissed with genome or DNA evidence is a fallacy for Weems. Prejudice requires neither a rational basis nor an evolutionary one. The artist readily acknowledges the power that race holds on our imaginations. But she asserts that differences within the human race are not, literally speaking, racial at all, that when we say race we mean nationality, or ethnicity, or religion, or culture, or class.[20]

The accompanying audio, titled *Let the Record Show*, provides both background and context for the photographic images, and works marvelously in tandem with classical and jazz composer James Newton's musical score.[21] Karen Sinsheimer, the curator of photography at the Santa Barbara Museum writes:

As scientists continue to unravel the strands of DNA, of which our human genome is constructed, Weems has woven threads of this factual information into her installation . . . in each of [her] fabric panels, images— some of which are appropriated—allude to a genetic truth. . . . In this artist-created theater of imagery, the viewer is wrapped in a harmonic space in which to contemplate the resulting human dilemmas created by our knowledge of genetics, that are taking center stage.[22]

Weems herself elaborates:

Biotechnology allows us to think about the future in new, exciting ways. At the same time, we have our real world that we have to understand in relationship to new discoveries. . . . For instance, look at where black people are in the culture. People say, 'They're so messed up—it must be genetic.' The idea that genes are connected to behavior carries potential for people to ignore the historical forces that bring people to what they are. The danger lies in assuming that this new science, along with computer technology, will put us all on a level playing field. That is a dangerous mistake because it doesn't. Who will have access to these amazing technologies? Will it be poor people or people with lots of cash? Right now, it's people with money. It's very classist and racist.[23]

Together, the images and narration in *The Jefferson Suites* raise complex and real issues. Weems is one who adheres to the belief that research into DNA and genetics presents new possibilities for progress as well as risks. Her installation reflects the heightened interest in how genetic information will become an "indisputable truth"—one that will not only have a profound effect on the future with cloning and medical and privacy issues, but also with revelations that can change the lives of everyone.[24]

The Hampton Project, Carrie Mae Weems's most recent commission, and her third and avowedly last fabric installation, holds singular meaning for Williams College. For although the exhibition is a showcase for the work of two women, distanced by time and race and joined by their discipline and focus on the Hampton Institute, Weems's piece presents a web of associations touching on Williams lore, alumni personality, and institutional philosophy, all set against the backdrop of a remarkable chapter in our nation's development. Drawing on historical fact and relying on over a century of retrospection, "The Hampton Project" establishes a contemporary discourse on issues of race and education, and it highlights the visual arts as capable of identifying and defining (racial) identity.

In 1996 the Williams College Museum of Art invited Weems to collaborate on a project dedicated to the history and legacy of the Hampton Normal and Agricultural Institute (now Hampton University), using Frances Benjamin Johnston's *Hampton Album* of 1900 as her point of departure. The resultant exhibition, *Carrie Mae Weems: The Hampton Project,* which opened in March 2000, bears witness to the language of photography as deftly applied to one artist's largely documentary vision of Hampton and to Weems's evocation of the institute as a site of recollection and reflection.

Located on the Chesapeake Bay in Hampton, Virginia, Hampton was founded by General Samuel Chapman Armstrong, a Williams College alumnus and charismatic commander of black troops during the Civil War, as an institution devoted to the education of African Americans and (after 1878) Native Americans. Subject to his guidance, the institute became a model vocational school with its mission to provide students with "an education for life" through a program structured to train "the head, the hand, and the heart." Academic course work, manual training, and Christian education were combined with the goal to produce graduates who would return to their own communities as both teachers and leaders. [25]

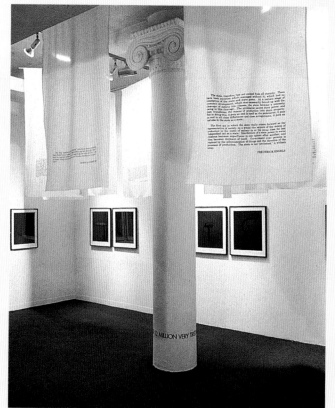

Installation view, "And 22 Million Very Tired and Very Angry People," The New Museum of Contemporary Art, New York, 1991

Armstrong (1839–1893) has been criticized—"a grand prevaricator," "paternalistic in the extreme," "a consummate racist," "a pragmatic accommodationist"—as well as loudly applauded for his philosophy and his efforts to create a model school and multiracial society at Hampton. In his sensitive essay in this book, Frederick Rudolph sorts through the complexities and contradictions of Armstrong—son of missionaries to the Sandwich Islands, Williams man (class of 1862), and brevet brigadier general at the close of the Civil War—who dedicated his life and considerable energies to ensuring the progress of black people after emancipation, as well as the welfare of nineteenth-century America's other forgotten community, Native Americans.

In December 1899, seven years after Armstrong's death, Frances Benjamin Johnston (1864–1952) received the commission to photograph the Hampton Normal and Agricultural Institute. [26] She was asked to provide a record of the campus, the student body, and, implicitly, "the progress" of education under the institute's influence for a public relations display at the 1900 Universal Exposition in Paris. In her essay on Johnston for this volume, Constance W. Glenn, director of the art museum at California State University, Long Beach, shares a full account of the photographer's career and her renowned Hampton project.

Johnston's pictures invite an assessment of Hampton, its ideologies, and its students. In examining her commissioned images, we gain some insight into the institute's overarching goal of assimilating African Americans and Native Americans into the white world of possibility. Current scholarship generally considers the photographs promotional, propagandist affidavits of the progress African Americans and Native Americans could make under "the Hampton method." But some analyses also emphasize a more political and socioeconomic theme: the imaging of African Americans and Native Americans as moral, educated, and regimented workers serving to assure whites of the continuing hegemony of the American (read Anglo-Saxon) dream and value system. Photographs showing students performing agricultural tasks and participating in traditional (white) extracurricular activities reassured whites that racial status would be maintained.

While the Johnston photographs can be read as perpetrating African American and Native American subordination within a white, capitalist society, they may also be seen as ennobling. The series can be interpreted as a positive visual document of two minorities in the face of stereotypes perpetuated by what historian Henry Louis Gates, Jr. has called "plantation fictions, blackface minstrelsy, vaudeville, racist pseudo-science, and vulgar Social Darwinism." [27] The pictures have also been thought of as a conscious effort by the photographer herself to comment on the conventions of Victorian society. [28]

In her own essay in this volume, Deborah Willis-Kennedy, exhibitions director of the Anacostia Museum and Center for African American History and Culture, Smithsonian Institution, comments on several of these issues and offers her further observations on Johnston's photographs and the intersection of the *Hampton Album* and the imagery of the "New Negro."

The Hush of Your Silence, from "Who What When Where," 1998

It is generally conceded that even documentary photographers are unable to provide neutral, objective, unbiased pictorial records, for every photographer brings to the process of creation a singular, cultural identity. In this day and age, we must acknowledge Johnston's documentary Hampton work, hauntingly "clear" as it seems to be, as propagandist by intent and, more importantly, imbued with the polemics of her culture; similarly, we must accept Weems's own Hampton project as informed by her background and personal manifesto.

Weems's commission is shaped in part as a response to historical photographs of the institute and period images of African Americans and Native Americans. Using a small selection of Johnston's pictures of the historically black university, Weems calls into question Johnston's ability as a photographer to portray truth and proceeds to appropriate her imagery in an attempt to give it new actuality. Weems then looks further than the Hampton campus, tapping myriad other photographic resources to relate initial contacts between Anglos, African Americans, and Native Americans, the institution of slavery, the Civil War and its aftermath, the juggernaut of Western expansion, the era of Jim Crow, the civil rights conflicts of our own century, and the land claim disputes of the present, gently embracing all within a multilayered work of elegiac significance. The balance of Weems's discourse within *The Hampton Project*, however, is ultimately her very personal response to the philosophy of Hampton's visionary founder and to historic and contemporary intersections of race, education, and the democratic ideal. [29]

Installation view, *Ritual & Revolution*,
Philip Morris Kunstförderung, 1998

Slave Coast, detail of triptych from *Ritual & Revolution*, 1993

Weems has explained that, for her, the institute was a metaphor, a point of departure from which she could explore ideas about education, democracy, and their mutual relationship. She has shared her personal view of Hampton, speaking to what she sees as the school's original goal of forcibly establishing a "heritage" for its pupils and bemoaning the ease with which that heritage superceded the cultural legacies of its black and Indian student body.[30]

Weems sees much of the American educational system as infected with decontextualized, disembodied, and irrelevant exercises that teach students to fake understanding and to seek a norm of approval rather than knowledge, comprehension, and creativity. In a recent newspaper interview, Weems shared that "[she doesn't] think [*The Hampton Project*] is really about Hampton . . . [and] it doesn't have only to do with African Americans or Native Americans. . . . It addresses the ways education can result in stamping out carbon copies, creating people with the same moral code, who find value in the same things."[31]

In a subsequent interview she continues this thought, "I felt very lucky when Williams called. . . . The exhibition is a wonderful opportunity to explore questions about education and repression. . . . The viewer is prompted to ask very critical questions about American history, personal

history, and personal responsibility. The exhibition is crafted that way, with sound, narrative, and text, and huge visual images. This questioning, examination, and critiquing are not ways to fix blame but are part of a process. Students here at Williams are engaged in education, and education is always about maintaining the status quo. It is based on conformity. And that becomes most obvious when we look at questions of education regarding people of color: Native Americans, African Americans. Will they be imbued with the values of Anglo culture; will they align themselves with Anglo culture?"[32]

Initially Weems's premise seems twofold: to remember and reflect upon the past with the purpose of "pulling it apart to see where the tangles exist,"[33] and to use that knowledge to provide for a future in which we willingly acknowledge, preserve, and celebrate diversity, our individual legacies. But, true to form (and with trademark belligerence), the artist pushes the envelope as she squares off against the crushing tides of history to provide a fresh way of looking at and protesting what she sees as the multifaceted oppression of African Americans and Native Americans. She does this by producing an experience that heightens the viewer's awareness of certain political and socioeconomic realities, forcing a

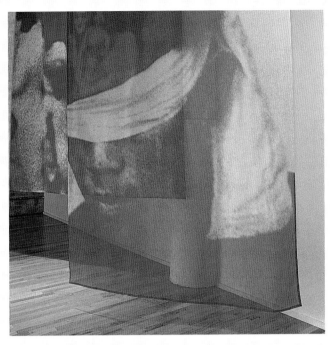

Detail from *Ritual & Revolution*, 1998

Installation view, *Ritual & Revolution*, P.P.O.W., 1998

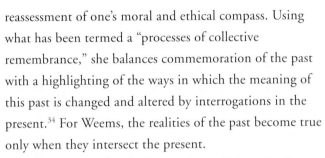

reassessment of one's moral and ethical compass. Using what has been termed a "processes of collective remembrance," she balances commemoration of the past with a highlighting of the ways in which the meaning of this past is changed and altered by interrogations in the present.[34] For Weems, the realities of the past become true only when they intersect the present.

This methodology and tactical use of history and commemoration is obviously present in *The Hampton Project*, and precedents can be found in Weems's work from the beginning. "Family Pictures and Stories" is an early example, as the artist juxtaposes and contrasts memories of people with present reality. In "And 22 Million Very Tired and Very Angry People," rather than investigating a shared history, the artist examines individuals aligned by their commitment to eliminate oppression and injustice and linked across space and time.[35] Weems's "Sea Islands Series," 1991-1992; two additional series of plates, "Went Looking for Africa" and "Landed in Africa" (both from 1991–1992); and the "Africa Series" (1993) all refer to a historicizing approach that noted cultural critic bell hooks has termed "diasporic landscapes of longing," and has linked with the artist's endeavor to reframe the black image and the idea of connectedness within a (subversive) politic

of representation that challenges the logic of racist colonization and dehumanization.[36]

Such an approach presupposes a particular and very individual vision of history. It is one that involves "creative remembrance," and redresses "the gaps and spaces in the history of the marginalized, [restores] subjugated knowledge, and [provides] a place for the unrecorded voices of the working class, of enslaved Africans, women, and the ghosts of the oppressed worldwide to be heard." [37]

Weems doesn't necessarily take liberties with the facts as she renders the implicit explicit; she simply refuses to ignore some of the gray areas of human experience in an effort to be fair and honest with the totality of historic truth. With her folklore and storytelling background, Weems would be the first to acknowledge the importance of fiction to our understanding of history; she knows that much of our awareness of the past derives from novels, staged photography, and alternative media.

One of the most provocative examples of Weems's creative use of history, (and of her ability to shape collective memory as a contemporary *griot*), can be found in her 1995 piece "From Here I Saw What Happened and I Cried." The work was commissioned by a pedigreed institution, the J. Paul Getty Museum, in response to an exhibition titled *Hidden Witness: African Americans in Early Photography*, presumably to encourage a contemporary reading of a selection of historic photographic images.[38]

Writing about this work in *Carrie Mae Weems: Recent Work, 1992–1998*, curator Thelma Golden claimed:

What Weems did was perhaps even more subversive than the institutionally sanctioned subversion inherent in the act of commissioning her. Her phototext installation created an alternative history that simultaneously embraced and rejected what the museum's photographs represented. Instead of exhibiting one of her own extant pieces, she courageously and critically read the museum's show through her own new series of works. She expressed that reading in her texts, which accompanied her photographs. In the vernacular, to read is to critique, to create a metadiscourse around an idea. It is to think and respond actively and acutely with wit and irony. Weems's piece is an incredible read. [39]

With "From Here I Saw…," Weems sketches a personal and emotional account of the history of Africans in America. She frames her story with two identical images of an African woman in profile, tinted blue, and with a text imposed on the first image reading, "FROM HERE I SAW WHAT HAPPENED," and on the closing (reversed) image, "AND I CRIED." Weems begins her narrative with four pictures taken from nineteenth-century anthropological studies of African Americans mounted in tondo form and printed in red. Over these Weems has etched "YOU BECAME A SCIENTIFIC PROFILE," "AN ANTHROPOLOGICAL DEBATE," "A NEGROID TYPE," "& A PHOTOGRAPHIC SUBJECT." Her next four images, treated similarly, brand comparable pictures of slaves with their type: "HOME," "YARD," "FIELD," and "KITCHEN." From here the artist moves from the past into the present, infusing her story of black history with instances of hatred and stereotyping as well as moments of resistance and survival. "She is as brilliant a writer as she is a manipulator of images, and she has seamlessly wedded language to the images she has found in archives and standard photo histories. Her rage is also in perfect balance with her rationality, an incendiary combination." [40]

For *The Hampton Project*, Weems has once again chosen to transfer digitized images of historic moments, sites, and individuals onto semitransparent muslin banners ranging in size from four-by- five to eight-by-ten feet, along with stretched canvases, arranging them floor to ceiling throughout the museum's Class of 1935 Gallery. She accentuates the narratives implied in her selection of photographs through her use of clustering and sequence, and she employs audio—an extended poetic narrative—as an evocative counterpoint to the imagery. The overlapping experiences of blacks and Indians are emphasized through a conceptual narrative, not a chronological account. She offers the viewer a text that addresses subject matter so culturally laden with history, tragedy, memory, notoriety, and myth that the end result is a work she herself says "aspires to emblematic resonance, and conveys rich associations beyond the art world into history, literature, universal custom and mores." [41]

As in the "Africa Series," "From Here I Saw What Happened and I Cried," and her two previous fabric suites, Weems has availed herself of images from the past through the present. She draws upon her immeasurable visual repertoire and appropriates only the most salient images to serve her multifaceted compositions. *The Hampton Project* is comprised of twenty-four documentary images, digitally rendered, and enlarged to life-size.[42] Weems's own photography exists side-by-side with nineteenth-century period pictures by William Larrabee, Frances B. Johnston, members of the Kiquotan Kamera Klub at the Hampton Institute, and anonymous pictures from the archives at both Hampton University and Williams College. A 1904 portrait by Edward Sheriff Curtis (of a Navajo god impersonator) hangs near images of a frontier Indian baptism from the collection of the Church of Latter-Day Saints and its modern thematic counterpart, a moment captured during the early sixties race riots in Birmingham, Alabama—the hosing of a group of African Americans. [43]

The artist's criteria for her photo selection must be that each image is as visually arresting as it is culturally laden. For instance, her choice of a detail from a photograph of Augustus Saint-Gaudens's Shaw Memorial in Boston is an inspired choice in light of its ability to reinforce the entire installation's multivalence. This is cerebral seduction at a high level. The Shaw Memorial was unveiled and ushered to public acclaim with impassioned dedication speeches (one by Booker T. Washington, Armstrong's protégé and Hampton's most famous graduate) in May 1897. "The monument commemorated the soldiers of the Fifty-fourth Massachusetts Volunteer Infantry Regiment—the first troop of black soldiers to have been permitted to enlist in the Union Army—and their white leader Colonel Robert Gould Shaw, who, along with many of his men, lost his life in battle.

While Shaw is central to the composition of the sculpture, his foot soldiers (who proved to skeptics that black men could be valiant soldiers) are given equal prominence. Never before had so many black people been honored in one American monument.[44] The parallels to Armstrong and his own dedication to "his men and his mission" are self-evident. Weems has chosen an image with wide historical and political reverberations; her selection also refers to the growing body of artwork at the turn of the century that was based more on positive depictions of the disenfranchised than on debilitating stereotypes.

Singer, from *The Jefferson Suites*, 1999

Another instance of cognitive serendipity involves the large banner depicting a tomb sculpture of a draped and reclining female nude, her elbow resting on several enormous bound volumes. The image is the result of Weems's travels through Pisa, Italy, where, struck by the work's extreme beauty and pensive tenor, she photographed it. Those intrinsic merits prompted her to include the picture in *The Hampton Project*. Only later did research reveal the identity of the memorial sculpture as that of Sappho, the Greek poetess known for her

eulogies, laments, and elegies, carved by Giovanni Dupré (1817–1882) for the sarcophagus of the natural philosopher Carlo Modotti. The essence of the sculpture, its origins aside, contributes to the tone of *The Hampton Project*; its history adds further nuance to the underlying themes of the work as a whole.

As a counterpoint to the hanging banners, Weems has incorporated five digitally enlarged period photographs transferred onto stretched canvas and hung high on the walls within the installation. The works depict the Hampton Institute's founder and his extended family on the porch of the principal's home, a group portrait of Native Americans soon after their arrival at Hampton in 1878, and then again in 1880, and two panels of a single image (one reversed) of brass band musicians.[45] The following text by Weems is superimposed on the center of the Armstrong family group portrait: "With your missionary might you extended the hand of grace reaching down and snatching me up and out of myself"—an oblique statement whose interpretation touches on questions of race and education as well as societal and religious ideologies that have inspired as well as perplexed, enraged, and divided Americans for over a century.

Massive appropriated photographs, digitally rendered onto stretched canvas, were featured in Weems's installation "Who What When Where" (1998). An image of graduating West Point cadets enthusiastically tossing their hats in the air carries the tag line "HIP-HIP HOORAY ONCE AGAIN CAPITALISM IS SAVED." Four additional canvasses present four sepia-toned still lifes of a typewriter, a book, a clock, and a globe; each one carries a one-word inscription: "WHO," "WHAT," "WHEN," and "WHERE"—all questions relevant to a narrative of political portent.[46]

To accentuate *The Hampton Project*'s comprehensive resonance and complex meaning, Weems quietly invokes other forms of expression with which the installation shares concerns and spirit. One such example is late nineteenth- and early twentieth-century literature, poetry, and philosophy, in particular W. E. B. Du Bois's book *The Souls of Black Folks* (1903),[47] that exhibits similar empathy with the plight of the African American (and by extension the Native American). Weems's choice of oversized photo-banners also subtly evokes the long-standing Native American pictographic tradition of narrative scenes of epic battles and histories on buffalo hides and tipis. In the later half of the nineteenth century and into the early twentieth, in the absence of skins, plain yard goods of muslin and canvas, along with paper, served similar documentary purposes.[48]

The Souls of Black Folks, a collection of fourteen powerful essays that stand

Installation view, *The Jefferson Suites*, 1999

as a mix of reportage and autobiography, is a layered portrait of the conditions facing recently emancipated African Americans at the turn of the century. In it, historian and sociologist Du Bois shares his prophetic statement, "The problem of the Twentieth Century is the problem of the color line"; and he introduces his influential concept of "double consciousness": the struggle of (African Americans) trying to define themselves as both black and American—of living with the "Veil of Race."[49] Weems mines this conceit, literally and figuratively, applying it to the situations of both the African American and the Native American within the framework of *The Hampton Project.*

The image *Old Folks at Home* in Weems's installation is another such example. As Constance Glenn notes in her essay on Frances B. Johnston, a few of the platinum prints in the original album cannot be attributed to Johnston; they are most likely ascribed to members of the institute's camera club. Indeed, the Kiquotan Kamera Klub was very active during the period 1893–1926, with its membership working with the aesthetic and technical guidance of well-known period photographers who visited the campus regularly.[50] Several of these collaborations resulted in published work, including illustrations to six out of a total of seven illustrated volumes of the poetry of noted African American author Paul Lawrence Dunbar (1872–1906). Dunbar, whose work deals with the vagaries of life, his poetry infused with wit, passion, fervor as well as melancholy, shares concerns raised in both Du Bois's ideology, as expressed in *The Souls of Black Folks*, and Weems's *Hampton Project*. Weems has acknowledged the importance of one Dunbar poem in particular: "We Wear the Mask." In light of her subtle use of the images of children wearing masks, the Navajo ceremonial figure, the Ku Klux Klan parade float "White Supremacy," the yearbook portraits of two proud Hampton seniors, not to mention Weems's own reference to black fraternities and sororities in her audio narrative, the associations of hiding, cultural masking, and accommodation evident in this installation are more than apt.[51]

Weems is critical of the institute's founding philosophies, their practical implementation, and the end results of what she sees as a flawed educational system prevalent at the turn of the century. Although initiated by the well-intentioned seeking to solve the black and Indian "problem" of the time in as humane a way as possible, that system, as made manifest at institutions such as the Hampton Normal and Agricultural Institute, subjected African Americans and Native Americans to every pressure of coerced assimilation.

For Weems, whose indignation is grounded in her own black and Indian heritage, the dilemma of the Native American proves a most poignant catalyst and signifier. She sees the reduction of individual Native-American peoples into a generalized melting pot as reducing many Indians to nothing at all, victims of racial supremacy, prevailing governmental politics, and economic advancement. Stripped of their religion, ideals, self-esteem, and identity, institution graduates, still alienated from or rebuffed by the white man's society and feeling insecure as Indians, fell into a limbo between two worlds, failing as "white" and no longer feeling comfortable on the reservation.[52]

Installation view, *The Jefferson Suites*, 1999

"Paradigm shifts in art historical studies remind us that simple one-to-one correspondences of image and historical event are infrequent. All historical representations are multivalent, their meanings accrue as they are made and used, as they change hands, as they become significant many years after their creation."[53] In a masterful stroke of revisionism, Weems capitalizes on the anonymity of the Native Americans prevalent in period pictures in her own effort to humanize and empower them. She exercises their lack of identity, divorcing them further from specific time and place to underscore the relevancy and timeless poignancy of Native American history and purpose. In Weems's worldview, no one—black or white—escapes culpability for the plight of the Indian: "Remember that the Indians who paved the way along with you/Were snatched up again and driven to the buffalo jump/The reserved lands reserved for a destitute and homeless people/And your marching band played on."[54]

Prefacing each chapter of *The Souls of Black Folks*, Du Bois includes a bar of rich lyrics from several African spirituals, which he calls "sorrow songs."[55] They "tell in word and music of trouble and exile, of strife and hiding; they grope towards some unseen power and sigh for a rest in the End."[56] Weems includes one banner centered within the framework of *The Hampton Project* that carries the following text: "From a great height I saw you falling/Black and Indian alike/and for you she played/a sorrow song." The overall composition includes a standing female figure, seen half-length and looking away from the viewer toward an image of David Wojnarowicz's *Buffalo Jump* (1988–89); the entire banner is tinted blue.[57] The ethereal figure is the artist herself, an omniscient observer to the inexorable and our mediator to those oppressed and disenfranchised souls conjured from the past.

Weems has inserted her own image within her work before: in "Untitled (The Kitchen Table Series)" where she assumes the role (and issues) of the contemporary African American woman; as *A Veiled Woman* from "And 22 Million Very Tired and Very Angry People," covering her

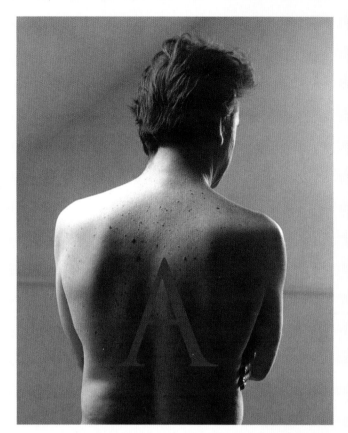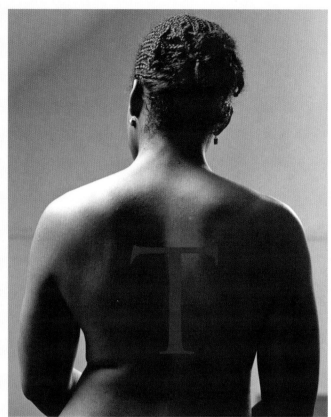

Above and opposite: DNA backs, from *The Jefferson Suites*, 1999

face to mask the horrors of the world; shrouded seductively on the paneled screen *The Apple of Adam's Eye*, and as the weeping *Woman in White* in a multipaneled grouping from the "Sea Islands Series." In *Ritual & Revolution*, a blue-tinted self-portrait banner promotes Weems "as a beatific pre-Hellenic goddess—a Black Athena. . . . An image," says art critic Ernest Larsen, ". . . clearly intended to decenter Western conceptions of history as the province of white men, and to refigure the traditionally male image of the artist in history."[58] Then in *The Jefferson Suites*, Weems becomes a singer, striking the pose of the chanteuse working within moody indigo surroundings to take center stage with her repertoire of melodies. Always strong, never pitying, her voice is one of transcendence and hope (for the benefits of expanded genetic study) as well as of resignation (in the face of the profound moral and ethical issues arising from this growing science). The lady can sing the blues.

Weems's own image works masterfully in tandem with her audio text, providing for the presence of an avatar assisting us to a collective consciousness and a comprehensive perception of history. The artist (as informed by her folklorist training) is particularly interested in language, not necessarily for its properties of definition, but more for its ability to speak to deeper themes without encumbering "the message" with issues grounded in the personal. This is crucial to her work as she sublimates the individual within the communal to engage the viewer in the notion of a universal human experience. This is evident in both *The Hampton Project* and in *Ritual & Revolution*, where Weems's extended audio narrative promotes the first person singular as the narrator of the text, nurturing that presence from individual participant into an omnipresent "I."[59] And as the artist has explained, it is also a feminine "I," with a woman symbolizing the compassionate being watching history unfold.[60]

To experience Weems's fabric suites is to be submerged in them, surrounded by layers of huge, shimmering images, becoming one with them. She explains, "I wanted to bring together the idea that none of us can be separated from history. . . . You can stand in the installations. They can be a place where you experience a deep level of contem-

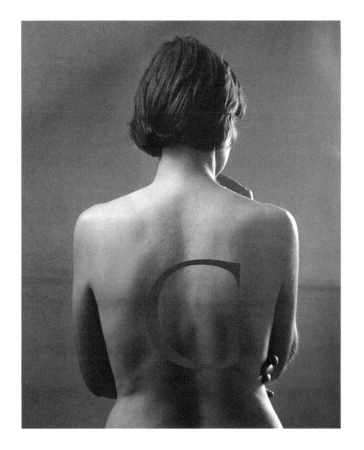 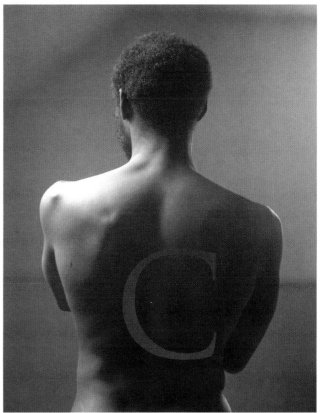

plation . . . they ask you to enter. . . . They demand that you physically and mentally immerse yourself." [61]

In *Ritual & Revolution*, the artist refers to the past with an examination of civilization and the struggle for cultural integrity, questioning whether social involvement can influence individual and communal development. In *The Jefferson Suites*, she looks to the past and to the future and ultimately to science with its promise for human advancement as well as its risks. In *The Hampton Project*, Weems returns to the present to underscore education as able to illuminate some of the great themes of history and as a vital key to contemporary discourse on social values and the hegemony of race and class.

Weems has embarked on a mission of beguiling visual warfare, appropriating, enlarging, annotating her images with the spoken word and written texts to bestow the very precious gift of a renewed public persona on those who have heretofore depended on others, or submitted to them, for dignified representation and subsequent empowerment. [62] Weems's trilogy of fabric works is at once as compelling in

its drama and evocation of tragedy, as it is expansive in its acknowledgment of tremendous human achievement.

As of this writing, Carrie Mae Weems is in residence on the Williams College campus as the Sterling A. Brown, [63] Class of 1922, Visiting Professor, teaching in the Art Department, and one cannot be but struck by the appropriateness of her tenure in this prestigious professorship. The similarities between Brown and Weems—the poet and the image-maker—are striking in their mutual adoption of aesthetic forms from black experience and tradition to establish texts and contexts that articulate a vision of the world that celebrates the dignity and worth of a people largely misunderstood and misrepresented. And ultimately, they both speak eloquently to the necessity and power of using one's voice in the cause of a humanistic vision rooted in democratic principles.

—VIVIAN PATTERSON
Associate Curator, Collections Management,
Williams College Museum of Art

Before Columbus and

the invention of the New World

before Stanley & Livingston

the Portuguese & the Dutch & King Leopold

Before the British, after the Revolution

and the exacting hand of tyranny

Before Jefferson's Democracy

& after Jackson's invading army

Before Lewis & Clark

and the Mason-Dixon Line

Before Manifest Destiny

The March of Industry

and after the opening of the West

Before the first trade beads

were traded

and after human flesh

was weighed in gold

Before King Cotton and Queen Rice

ounce for ounce for ounce

and after the blue notes of indigo &

Before the Trail of Tears and

the red Cherokee Rose

after the mise en scène

Before your resistance and

of the Middle Passage

after you knew you fought

before you became

the same ole men, the same ole men

labor and capital combined

who thought the world was flat

and the source of vast vacant lands

Before you tilled the soil into the ground

And after you became

and after your bodies were no longer useful

the key in the Mother of Invention

Before you were freed &

spinning Ginny's cotton into gold

after an assassin's bullet

Before clandestine operations

covert actions and the

maddening twist of your slaughter

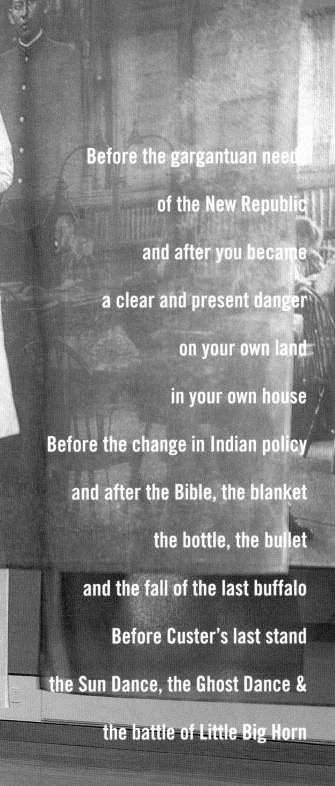

Before the gargantuan needs

of the New Republic

and after you became

a clear and present danger

on your own land

in your own house

Before the change in Indian policy

and after the Bible, the blanket

the bottle, the bullet

and the fall of the last buffalo

Before Custer's last stand

the Sun Dance, the Ghost Dance &

the battle of Little Big Horn

Before the reign of terror

and the nights of vengeance

and after the smoke cleared
Before Wild West Shows
and the dust settled
minstrel shows & circus acts and
After Sitting Bull
after your clowning days were over
After Crazy Horse
Before Indian head nickels
your loss of meaning
& buffalo dimes
your permanent fixing
Before the Washington Red Skins
and the scattering of your tribe
the Atlanta Braves
And long before you forgot
& the Cleveland Indians
what was what & who was who

Lakota Dahomey

Seminole Sioux

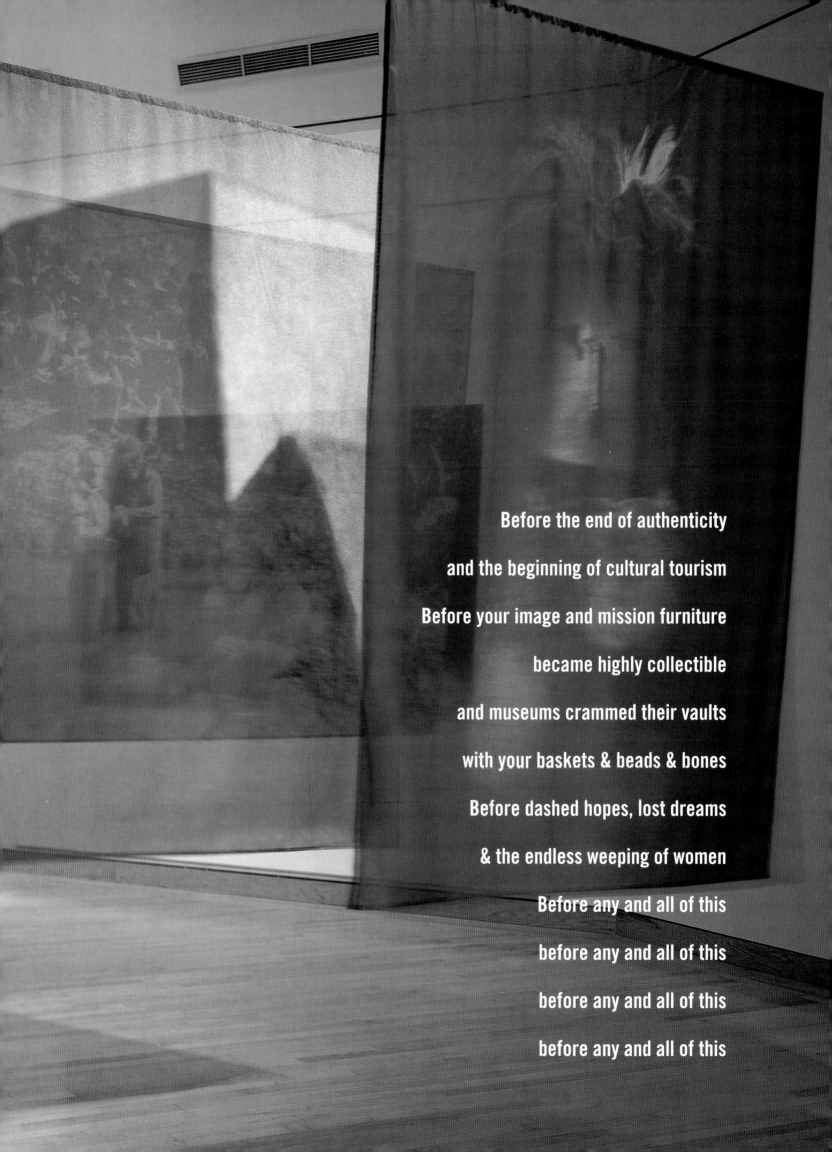

Before the end of authenticity

and the beginning of cultural tourism

Before your image and mission furniture

became highly collectible

and museums crammed their vaults

with your baskets & beads & bones

Before dashed hopes, lost dreams

& the endless weeping of women

Before any and all of this

before any and all of this

before any and all of this

before any and all of this

SAMUEL CHAPMAN ARMSTRONG:
Founder of the Hampton Institute

Less than a century after the Declaration of Independence, the United States abandoned one of its fundamental, if controversial, institutions by abolishing slavery. Not that it altogether knew what it was doing. Emancipation was not a carefully considered plan of action, taking into account the vast economic, political, social, and psychological changes it would visit upon the freedmen, their former owners, upon the whole fabric of a society that was feeling its way toward a confident nationhood. As it happened, emancipation was an accident of war.

Emancipation therefore thrust a sudden and unavoidable question upon a nation that did not want to answer it; nor, in the end, did it know how. That question was what to do for and about four million black Americans now that they were no longer slaves.

One person who did know what ought to be done was Samuel Chapman Armstrong, a young foreigner who graduated from Williams College in 1862. Armstrong, the son of American missionaries to the Sandwich Islands, was born on the island of Maui in 1839; the next year his family moved to Honolulu, where he was reared in a multiracial society while his parents, as was sometimes said of the missionaries, busied themselves making Puritans out of Polynesians. Armstrong would have been something of a dullard had he not recognized in the Christian paternalism of his missionary parents a guide to one answer for the question that now bedeviled his adopted country.

Since 1820, New England missionaries had been trying against great odds to turn Pacific atolls into outposts of New England religion, polity, and values. Richard Armstrong, Sam's father, was the islands' minister of education and pastor of the Honolulu church charged with bringing the local people into the Christian fold and holding them there. The Polynesians of the Hawaiian Islands, as the Sandwich Islands were also known, were attractive and pleasant people, but they were also uncomplicated and indolent, and, in the eyes of New England missionaries, candidates for moral guidance and discipline.

Whether in the simple, direct message of the hymn "Work, for the Night Is Coming," or in the intricacies of Puritan theology, work is central to the definition of Christian character and worthiness. Work was central to the missionaries' efforts to enlighten an unsophisticated people who had not yet experienced Western Christian culture and who appeared to live simple lives of comfortable laziness and erotic pleasure. Work not only tamed unruly passions, it also brought forth the skills and self-confidence on which economic independence and moral responsibility rested.

The Hawaiian missionaries gave land to those who lived on it, focused on educating a leadership class, taught women how to strengthen their role as moral guides, and combined rudimentary liberal learning with labor. Richard Armstrong started the first sawmills and sugar plantations on Maui as incentives to industry. Sam accompanied him by foot and canoe on school inspection trips. By 1859, while a student at Punahou College, Sam was editor of the Hawaiian-language newspaper in Honolulu. He accepted without question the arrangements that made New England missionaries the mentors, the patrons, and therefore to some degree the servants of Christian Polynesians.

Sam Armstrong arrived at Williams College (in Williamstown, Massachusetts) during winter vacation in December 1860, three months after his father had died from a riding accident. His father had wanted him to transfer from Punahou in order to experience the teaching and inspiration of the college's president, Mark Hopkins. Richard Armstrong and Hopkins were colleagues on the American Board of Commissioners for Foreign Missions, the missionary arm of the Congregational churches. Although he preferred Yale, Sam, an obedient and respectful son, entered Williams in January 1861. By the time of his graduation, he was writing to his mother: "I can never be too thankful that I came to Williams." [1]

Williams was a "natural" destination for missionary sons (Sam was one of three in the class of 1862). The legendary Haystack incident of 1860,[2] free tuition, and the reputation of Hopkins were expected to offset the realities of Williams College for a young man who was remembered by one of his contemporaries as "an islander" whose "constitution smacked of the salt sea. There was about him the high courage and the jollity of the tar."[3]

No sooner had Sam arrived in Williamstown than he was informing his family that "the mountains here are nothing more than nature's warts, little stuck-up hills that you could cross in an hour on a donkey going backward." Yet, in the same letter, he reported: "I had my first sleigh ride."[4] Four months later, however, he was an unhappy Hawaiian out of water: "I hope to get a swim in a month or two. In this miserable hole one can go into the stream only three months in the year. Not before the Fourth of July."[5] A few weeks earlier Sam's mood had been more exultant. He had gone to Albany with about sixty fellow students to see "Lincoln, the new President . . . [who] made a short speech. . . . he speaks like a man who means what he says and bends backwards and throws his body forward precisely as father used to when he spoke."[6]

Williams College justified Richard Armstrong's selection of a college for his son. A friendship developed with a classmate, Archibald Hopkins, son of the president. In the spring of 1861, Sam moved into the president's house as Archie Hopkins's roommate and thus began more than a year of informal friendly conversation and proximity to Mark Hopkins and his family. As his senior year began, Sam explained to his mother the importance of Hopkins's course in moral philosophy that brought his Williams education to a solemn climax: "The coming year . . . must tell heavily on our after lives; . . . we are treated like and feel like men now, and must quit ourselves like men. Soon the greatest mind in New England will take and train us."[7]

If Hopkins's was not the greatest mind in New England, it was, at least, for the purposes for which Richard Armstrong had sent his son to Williams: that he be ready to take on the world as a good man, ambitious and God-

serving. Sam himself looked "forward with joy to a life of doing good," but hesitated to commit himself to the ministry. "I mean to have good times after all and not to look like a galvanized mummy."[8] Indeed it is difficult to imagine the Sam Armstrong remembered by his classmates anywhere near a theological seminary: "He carried an air of insolent health, his nervous energy was volcanic, he was a cyclone under a felt hat. When he fenced with you, he seemed not only to cover the ground on every side but to occupy the air also. . . . He stood about five ten, erect, muscular, broad-shouldered, with large well-poised head, face thoughtful but rather combative and deeply bronzed by the South Seas. . . ."[9] On the other hand, there is no reason to believe that Sam questioned the principles that Hopkins's philosophy promoted: respect for property and the industry that ensured it, material success as an indication of moral character, particularly for those who translated their good fortune into good works. "Whatever good teaching I have done has been Mark Hopkins teaching through me," Sam Armstrong would remark later in life.[10] Any New Englander understood what Richard Armstrong meant when he said that lazy Hawaiians could be made moral if they could be made industrious. Mark Hopkins dressed the same message in more formal language and gave it a wider application. The young graduate who left Williamstown for a regiment of New York volunteers in August 1862 had come a long distance from home, and found his father and the values of the Christian community of Hawaii wonderfully confirmed.

Sam Armstrong's thinking may not have been significantly changed by his Williams experiences, but his style surely was. Soon after moving into the Hopkins household, he wrote his mother: "While in college I wish to be dressed as well as the best. . . . I find it pleasanter to be received as an equal . . . when I meet with the well-dressed of New York and even Williamstown."[11] This vital, impish, vigorous Hawaiian boy studied more than the curriculum while at college. He achieved a degree of cosmopolitan finish by associating with worldly Williams students, participating in

Above: Anonymous, *Samuel Chapman Armstrong*, ca. 1890

campus activities, and visiting Eastern cities during vacations. The young Armstrong already knew how to wear shoes when he arrived in Williamstown, although he never lost a fondness for the shoeless days and activities of Hawaii. When he left Williamstown he was sophisticated, self-confident, and bursting with promise. Sam Armstrong graduated fifth in his class, behind four valedictorians of New England preparatory schools.

The Williams connection never withered. In 1865, on leave from service during the war, he visited the Hopkins family for ten days. By November 1866, his colleagues at the experiment with education for the freedmen at Hampton included three class of 1862 classmates, soon to be joined by another, Archie Hopkins. In 1869 a committee charged with assisting Hampton in its public relations was chaired by Mark Hopkins and issued a ringing endorsement of Armstrong's policies and plans. Three of the four committee members were Williams alumni. In October 1869, Mark Hopkins conducted the wedding ceremony in Stockbridge, Massachusetts, that united Sam Armstrong and Emma Walker of that place. In 1887 the college awarded him an honorary degree.

Samuel Chapman Armstrong to some degree drifted into the events that created the Hampton Normal and Agricultural Institute. On the other hand, at key moments in that history he became a decisive and determined participant in the effort to provide leadership to a wobbling cause.

Armstrong thought of himself as a native of the Sandwich Islands, not as an American. He went to war under the influence of classmates, taking the path of least resistance, not as an American patriot, nor as a partisan on the slavery question. Once enlisted, however, he eventually found a passionate purpose. In an early letter from the Army, he referred to himself as "a sort of abolitionist . . . [who hasn't] learned to love the Negro. . . . I go for freeing them more on account of their souls than their bodies."[12] Experience with Negroes in any number did not occur until

after the Emancipation Proclamation of January 1, 1863, which gave the war a new purpose and Armstrong a cause that fully engaged him. In November 1863, at his request, he was appointed lieutenant colonel in the Ninth U.S. Colored Troops. The war transformed an immigrant college boy into an American, a proven leader of men who had found a calling: the welfare of the emancipated Negro. The kernel of the Hampton Institute and the educational philosophy that defined it were explicit in the letter with which he applied, at war's end, for an appointment to the Freedmen's Bureau: "My thought and sympathies are now chiefly with the large masses of colored people in this country who need to be educated and elevated; and who especially need earnest and active friends to see that they receive justice, to counsel and direct them, to gather up the rising generation in schools, and to encourage the . . . colored population to industry."[13]

How these thoughts and sympathies were translated into the Hampton Institute and, through his most famous student, Booker T. Washington, into the Tuskegee Institute as well, is beyond the reach of this essay. So is the strange experiment, beginning in 1878 with fifteen warriors captured in Oklahoma, that tried unsuccessfully for forty-five years to prepare Native Americans for a society that refused to accept them. Armstrong knew what to do but nonetheless underestimated the ways in which Republican politicians, racism Northern and Southern, and the faintheartedness of many of his supporters would undermine his efforts.

Confronted in the mass, as indeed they had to be in the milling throngs that congregated in the Hampton Roads area of Virginia when the war ended, the freedmen presented a bleak picture of ignorance, poverty, untidiness, lack of personal cleanliness, and absence of aspiration and ambition. Yet Armstrong knew what to do. Four million former slaves, he concluded, needed more than the traditional three Rs of a village school, more than the general education of an

Anonymous, Hampton Normal and
Agricultural Institute, Class of 1893

academy. The freedmen, Armstrong argued, needed an education focused on making a living as independent, self-sufficient human beings, and they needed an institution that would turn out black teachers to show the way. (Like homesteaders, timber interests, and railroads that were granted it, they also surely needed land, which was not forthcoming.)

The so-called industrial education through which Armstrong tried to give his students, and theirs, the tools to establish themselves in an uncaring world was an optimistic, perhaps self-deceiving, solution to a national problem that also lay in the hands of many others. Many efforts to provide schooling for the freedmen failed. Armstrong's efforts succeeded because he had chosen them as his life's work. He didn't give up, and died from overwork at fifty-four.

It is easy enough not to understand the educational philosophy of Hampton under Armstrong, particularly if one does not want to. James A. Garfield, Williams class of 1859, an incorporator of Hampton and a member of its original board, was himself skeptical of the industrial focus, remembering how manual training in Northern colleges had become a source of ridicule. He also was concerned about the relative neglect of what W.E.B. DuBois later referred to as "the talented tenth," yet he recognized the crisis that challenged Armstrong and the appropriateness of his response: "The first want of the freed people of the South is to know how to live and how to work."[14] Armstrong himself acknowledged the constraints that prevented miracles: "Our problem is how to skip three centuries in the line of development and to atone for the loss and injustices of ages."[15]

Armstrong had been dead seven years when Frances B. Johnston's *Hampton Album* of 1900 was published. With understanding and imagination, anyone looking at these photographs sees not only a well-scrubbed class of servants and semiskilled mechanics. There are also glimpses here of illiterate, unskilled, barefoot slave ancestors and middle-class professional black descendants. The Johnston album documents the essential message of Armstrong and Hampton: Work is the path to character and economic independence.

By 1900 Booker T. Washington and Tuskegee in Alabama had replaced Armstrong and Hampton in the public eye. In the words of Armstrong's most recent biographer, Armstrong had made Washington, "a black man, his spiritual heir and the bearer of his vision for the people to whom he had chosen to dedicate his life." In 1881, when Armstrong was asked to recommend a white man to lead the new normal school planned at Tuskegee, the only name he proposed was that of Booker T. Washington.[16] Two of the last months of his life, although partially paralyzed, he spent with Washington at Tuskegee, basking in a shared affection and acknowledging the interdependence of their work. Reminiscent of James A. Garfield's aphorism, "The ideal college is Mark Hopkins on one end of a log and a student on the other." Washington in *Up From Slavery* paid a comparable tribute to Armstrong: "One might have removed from Hampton all the buildings, class-rooms, teachers, and industries, and given the men and women there the opportunity of coming into daily contact with General Armstrong, and that alone would have been a liberal education."[17]

The story of Hampton and its counterparts elsewhere is a story of frustrated good intentions, rather than one of triumphant bad intentions. By the time of *The Hampton Album*, Armstrong's school and the others had run into the wall of hostility and indifference of racist America. Hampton could not lead people—Southern whites and disillusioned Northern liberals—where they did not want to go. What it did do was what Armstrong promised at the beginning: "I stand now where I have long aimed to stand. I can say to any noble, aspiring, whole-souled colored youth, of either sex in the South, 'here you can come, ragged and poor as you are, and become the man and woman you wish to become.' "[18]

Well might Mary Melvin, an 1874 graduate, remark, "As it is now, no one can keep the best things from me. And I owe all of this to Hampton."[19] At a time when the white population of the United States was being educated on the job and on the farm (and not too well at that), when immigrant children in the cities were being taught how to use a toothbrush but not much in the way of useful skills, the industrial education of Hampton and Tuskegee was in some ways superior to the alternatives generally available to ordinary white Americans.

—FREDERICK RUDOLPH
*Mark Hopkins Professor of History,
Emeritus, Williams College*

FRANCES B. JOHNSTON:
The Hampton Album

"Miss Johnston is a lady . . . she does good work."
— *Theodore Roosevelt*

Here were the ravishing images—almost a half-century old—coupled with the fateful coincidence that the discovery belonged not to some passing collector of Victorian ephemera, but to one of the few individuals of the period who held in his hands the ability to resuscitate the photographer's status. What a stunning find *The Hampton Album* was!

Frances Benjamin Johnston's 1899 photographs of the Hampton Normal and Agricultural Institute—grouped and titled, apparently, as they had been displayed in the *Exhibit of American Negroes* at the 1900 Universal Exposition in Paris—were found during World War II in a Washington, D.C. bookshop by the critic, connoisseur, and arts impresario Lincoln Kirstein. Some twenty years later, Kirstein made a gift of the "plump, anonymous, leather-bound album, old and scuffed"[1] to the Museum of Modern Art. Thus, in 1966, fourteen years after her death, Johnston was rescued from the art world's perimeter with MoMA's exhibition of 44 of the 159 original platinum prints and their simultaneous publication in Kirstein's catalog titled *The Hampton Album.*[2]

The self-styled "greatest woman photographer in the world"[3] had in fact enjoyed a busy, hugely diverse, and much-honored career of more than sixty years when she died in New Orleans in 1952, still a "holy terror," as hearsay would have it. Born in Grafton, West Virginia, Johnston grew up in New York City, Rochester, and lastly Washington, D.C., where her father worked for the Treasury Department. Following her graduation from Notre Dame Convent in Govanston, Maryland, in 1883, she set out, at nineteen, to study art at the fashionable Académie Julien in Paris. Returning to Washington in 1885, Johnston became one of the organizers of the Art Students League (later absorbed into the Corcoran Gallery School) and immediately began creating illustrations—drawings

and photographs—which were published through her New York press group affiliation. Her only formal instruction in photography was provided by Thomas William Smillie, director of the Smithsonian Institution's Division of Photography, and it was through his auspices that she received a Smithsonian letter of introduction that allowed her to travel and view photographs in Europe in 1890. Johnston had already developed lucrative relationships with such popular periodicals as *Ladies Home Journal, Demorest's Family Magazine, Harper's Weekly,* and the *Illustrated American,* and by 1894 business was so good that she decided to give up the bathroom darkroom in her parents' house and build her own studio. Added to the rear of their home at 1332 V Street, it was designed by the prominent architectural firm of Hornblower and Marshall, and had it survived to this day, it would look remarkably contemporary.

Favored with her own place of business and her family's impeccable Washington connections, Johnston prospered. The portrait studio, in particular, flourished as she became the photographer of choice to five presidential administrations—those of Grover Cleveland, Benjamin Harrison, William McKinley, Theodore Roosevelt, and William Howard Taft. In the end, *Life* magazine referred to her as "the closest thing to an official court photographer the United States has ever had."[4] This against all odds: Johnston was an unmarried, well-bred (if unconventional) young woman whose proper place—according to turn-of-the-century mores—was in the home.

No doubt because of her growing professional reputation, Johnston was commissioned to photograph a number of Washington public schools for the 1900 Paris Exposition. During six weeks in 1899, she made more than seven hundred negatives at various D.C. schools and, perhaps because of this experience, in December she received the assignment to photograph the Hampton Institute in Virginia. She was asked to provide a record of the campus and the student body for a public relations display also destined for the Paris fair.

It is upon this last project, undertaken in the final weeks of the nineteenth century, that Frances Benjamin Johnston's fame rests today. Foreshadowing her later work as an architectural photographer, the Hampton images are constructs; they are studies in the architecture of figure placement, frozen tableaux designed to enhance—as requested—the image of "progressive" education at Hampton. "In them," Lincoln Kirstein wrote, "hearts beat, breath is held; time ticks. Eyelids barely flutter. Outside of Hampton there is an ogre's world of cruel competition and insensate violence, but while we are here, all fair words that have been spoken to the outcast and injured are true. Promises are kept. Hers is the promised land."[5] Here Kirstein alludes not only to the airless stillness of the images, he touches on their utopian quality.

To many, especially founder Samuel Chapman Armstrong and his academic heirs, the Hampton Institute embodied the American dream: children of slaves would, through vocational education, rise to become proud, useful citizens.

Frances B. Johnston, Self-portrait (as "New Woman"), ca. 1896

Reexamining the Hampton photographs in 1998, art historian Jeannene M. Przyblyski proposed that "amid a broad variety of cultural work" they had to engage, these images "were intended to assure an American audience that free blacks could still be counted on to take their place in the agricultural economy of the South. They were meant to reassure an international community that the United States had its 'Negro problem' firmly in hand."[6] This may well have been the case in the broadest context. The images themselves, however, suggest that on the Hampton campus there was simply a uniform desire (among students, faculty, and staff) to honor the public relations assignment through displaying pride, accomplishment, diversity of learning experiences, and industrious activity. At least this is what Johnston's lens reflects.

By 1900 the Hampton myth was already beginning to crumble. The great exodus to the industrial North had begun, as the South festered with racial unrest. Writers have suggested that under the circumstances, Johnston went out of her way to settle a notable aura of peace and order on these particular images. Critic James Guimond notes that "In order to dramatize the belief that this dream was . . . a reality . . . Johnston . . . *arranged* [italics mine] her images to document the process that was supposed to change . . . slaves and wild Indians into self-respecting, self-supporting Americans."[7] On the other hand, historian Laura Wexler sees a reflection of Johnston's own open rebellion against Victorian conventions, proposing that because her self-portraits "mock" proper deportment "she could not have given the kind of education she saw at Hampton her unreserved approbation," and her "own ambivalence toward what she saw at Hampton is one reason that the photographs are so powerful."[8]

While there is every reason to reexamine these images in the light of current thinking, which has long discarded the original Hampton model, reading Johnston's photographs in a sociopolitical context of her design, when we know little or nothing of her intellectual and political passions, is daunting. Attributing a specific agenda to this body of work—other than that which came with the assignment—becomes an exercise in relying upon today's viewers to invent the meaning of the images. We can, however, bring what we know to the work. Johnston was first and foremost a journalist, and all of her school images (Hampton and

Frances B. Johnston, *Class in American History*, ca. 1900

Frances B. Johnston, *Arithmetic: Measuring and Pacing*, ca. 1899–1900

others) share compositional devices that imbue them with the formal beauty that, by her own admission, she sought in her art, and that Kirstein recognized in his discovery. Her group compositions, here and elsewhere, are linear, horizontal, and rely on either friezelike groupings, as in *Arithmetic: Measuring and Pacing*, or the diagonal, pyramidlike arrangements that distinguish *Trade School: Brick-laying* and *Stairway of Treasurer's Residence: Students at Work*, her signature image. Almost without exception, figures are turned inward, glancing back, or inclined in parentheses to bracket the scenes. The eyes seldom look at us; they look instead at the point where Johnston wishes us to focus—at the heart of the activity. The viewer's feeling is one of examining—if always removed from—a carefully staged tableau not unlike those posed theatricals that became popular turn-of-the-century parlor entertainment. When larger groups are pictured, figures are assembled in wedge formations that lead the eye to a central figure or point within or just beyond the frame. Nothing is left to chance. Nothing is spontaneous. We do find Johnston's aesthetic, if not her agenda, in the scrupulously framed scenes she has choreographed in the serenity of the white December light that she harnessed to establish intense contrasts and pictorial density. In concert, we find the heart of the Hampton Institute in the way the players have come costumed for her, and in their complicity in achieving her vision.

The pictures themselves were hugely successful in Paris (where Johnston also organized an exhibition of work by

American women photographers for the Third International Photographic Congress), and after their display in the fair at the Palace of Social Economy, they were shown at the Pan American Exposition of 1901 in Buffalo and in stereopticon format at a series of lectures in New York, Boston, and Philadelphia. Johnston herself received a gold medal for her photo essay on American schools, and a grand prix for her photographs of the Hampton Institute.

Following the Hampton commission, Johnston's career in photojournalism and portrait photography continued to thrive through the first decade of the new century, after which she shifted her attention to architectural and garden work. With her friend Mattie Edwards Hewitt, from 1913 to 1917 she kept a studio on Fifth Avenue in Manhattan, where their long list of distinguished clients included the architectural firms of McKim, Mead, and White, and Carrere and Hastings, as well as business barons J. P. Morgan and John Jacob Astor.

By 1920 Johnston had become a popular lecturer on gardens and "wrote in that year that she was beginning a tour from Cleveland through the Middle West into California."[9] At the same time she had begun to explore color photography and developed early expertise in color processing. Whether it was merely an act of closing one chapter in her life and beginning anew, or an effort to raise funds to support her new passions, in 1924 Johnston wrote to the Huntington Library in San Marino, California, offering to sell Henry E. Huntington her work that

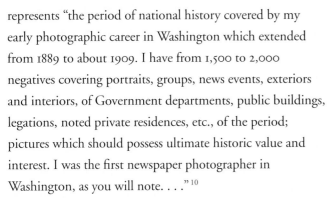

Frances B. Johnston, *Stairway of the Treasurer's Residence, Students Work*, ca. 1899–1900

Frances B. Johnston, *A Class in Dressmaking*, ca. 1900

represents "the period of national history covered by my early photographic career in Washington which extended from 1889 to about 1909. I have from 1,500 to 2,000 negatives covering portraits, groups, news events, exteriors and interiors, of Government departments, public buildings, legations, noted private residences, etc., of the period; pictures which should possess ultimate historic value and interest. I was the first newspaper photographer in Washington, as you will note. . . ."[10]

The price for the collection in its entirety (which did not include the school commissions) was $3,500, and Huntington did indeed make the purchase. The glass-plate negatives, along with a cyanotype proof file and a number of original prints, remain in San Marino today. Johnston went on to document historic gardens and architecture of the South with repeated funding from the Carnegie Foundation, and in 1945 she was made an honorary member of the American Institute of Architects. The largest archive of her work—more than 20,000 prints, 3,700 negatives, and 17,000 manuscript holdings—was acquired by gift of the artist and purchased from her estate by the Library of Congress.

Frances Johnston worked her entire adult life. She was a supremely self-confident woman and artist, never hesitating on either side of the art/journalism tightrope to claim her rewards. In Alfred Stieglitz's Photo-Secession (whose work she collected, focusing on the women photographers) she was recognized by her peers, as well as by presidents and tycoons, and she as a rule seemed to prefer those who

pushed the envelope. Look, for evidence, at one of her 1906 portraits of the renowned author Frances Hodgson Burnett, posed on the grounds of Maytham Hall, Burnett's estate in England.[11] At fifty-seven, Burnett vamps in an outrageous feather hat, contrasted against a faux-demure gesture, seemingly oblivious to the fact that the photographer has staked her elaborate gown into the foliage in order to create sharp compositional lines.

If the temper of her arresting portraits echoes the temper of the subject, Johnston herself is revealed in her depictions of equally unconventional women: "Princess Alice" Roosevelt, Teddy's brilliant, obstreperous daughter; Countess Marguerite Cassini (who drove a red sports car when other women looked forward to outings in horse-drawn carriages); and the eighty-year-old, utterly regal queen of suffragettes, Susan B. Anthony.[12] These portraits, coupled with images from thousands of news assignments, crowned by the radiant Hampton pictures, personify the working photographer whose pictures have transcended both their circumstances and hers. As Theodore Roosevelt said, entreating Admiral George Dewey to allow Johnston to photograph aboard the ships of the fleet after the battle of Manila Bay: "My dear Admiral . . . Miss Johnston is a lady . . . she does good work, and any promise she makes she will keep."[13]

—CONSTANCE W. GLENN
Director, University Art Museum,
California State University, Long Beach

VISUALIZING THE "NEW NEGRO"

As I collect, document, and talk about images of black America with diverse audiences, I realize that most viewers are intrigued with the range of imagery in the visual history, especially on black college campuses. Evidenced among this visual legacy of blacks are the photographs, which are often used by black people to combat racist representations of themselves. Not evident in the general photographic histories, black people at the time were indeed concerned about how they were portrayed. Photographs found in family collections and black college archives refute the visual stereotyping of black subjects. The dominant culture's representation of blacks in photography during the mid-1800s consisted largely of racist imagery and negative depictions. One need only peruse the visual representations of black subjects commonly produced on postcards and sheet music. The exaggerated features and demeaning situations they show made a negative impact that has endured to this day.

Photographs in collections of historically black college campuses are a paradox, as they visualize how race and gender is imagined in racial discourse. These photographs document the physical campus, its buildings, classrooms, teachers, and student activities. Most of the images depict students hard at work. The presidents, staff, faculty, and student portraits stress dignity and earnestness. Some selected photographs of the Hampton Institute were put on display at the Paris Exposition in 1900. Frances Benjamin Johnston's *Hampton Album*, which won the Grand Prix at the exposition, documented all aspects of campus life and was eventually exhibited and published as a book. African American photographer Harry Shepherd also presented his photographs of Hampton in the American Negro Exhibit at the exposition. Leigh Richmond Miner, who in 1907 was director of applied arts for the school, displayed photographs at the Jamestown tercentennial exposition. As art historian Richard Powell explained in his essay "To Conserve a Legacy: American Art from Historically Black Colleges and Universities," the visual message focused on the training of "the head, the hand, and the heart," specializing in the learning of a trade for service and

spirituality.[1] Somehow these images challenged the core problem of racism. The photographs consisted of young black men and women in the classroom, less than thirty years after emancipation. It is remarkable that the young black Americans posing for photographers such as Shepherd, Minor, and Johnston were either previously enslaved or descendants of enslaved men and women who worked in the fields and kitchens as laborers, artisans, and craftsmen. Yet they were photographed "learning a trade" that I would argue was taught to at least one of them by an elder. What these photographs characterized in their visual perception of black Americans was the origin of the look by the "other." Each subject could be viewed as acceptable in service to others. The photographs offer alternative ways of seeing and examining work—labor as it is "performed" in the photographs by each of the subjects.

This essay attempts to look at the cultural and visual history of young African Americans in photography during a critical year in the medium's first century, 1900. It also addresses the larger black community, as documented by black and white photographers. Race and power guide the photography of the Hampton images. Photographic images work reflexively, they both incite and help us imagine. Perhaps the most important aspect of my thesis is that racism is insidious. Glenn Jordan and Chris Weedon observe that "It is not simply that it [racism] provides justification for economic exploitation and political domination. If that were all racism did, its victims could live with it. The problem is that racism penetrates to the very core of who we are. It is one of the primary influences negating—or affirming—our sense of individual and group worth, passing final judgement on the value of one's history, culture and language, of one's intellect and physical appearance."[2]

The most discussed images of blacks are stereotyped as "the primitive," "the mammy," and minstrel performers. They are also seen as laborers or servants. As Ann Douglas writes, "It is one thing to be in search of the 'primitive' as white artists of the 1920s were; another thing to be told . . . that you are the primitive, the savage 'id' of Freud's new psychoanalytic discourse, trailing clouds of barbaric, prehistoric, preliterate 'folk' culture wherever you go."[3] The photographs of the Hampton students give the viewer a sense of the double consciousness in which the images worked for the subject as image-maker for the black race and markers for the goodwill and public relations of the institute. In a sense, the images transformed what Douglas describes as the "primitive" into the "civilized," countering Frederick Douglass's attack on the 1893 World's Colombian Exposition in which he criticized the organizers for exhibiting "the Negro as a repulsive savage."[4] The expressive power of these photographic images, serving as documentary and artistic works and political and public relations propaganda, is still significant, as they provide a visual record of the education of blacks in this country.

At the turn of the century, photography expanded in a variety of ways. Newspapers, journals, and books published photographic images. Courses in photography were offered in schools and colleges, and correspondence courses were available. It was also a period defined as the time of the "New Negro" by artists, educators, historians, and philosophers. Yet a large number of stereotypical images produced by the dominant culture depicted black men, women, and children as caricatures.

As reported by historian Cary D. Wintz, the term "New Negro" was first used on June 28, 1895, in an editorial in the *Cleveland Gazette* about the "new class of blacks with education, class, and money that had arisen since the Civil War."[5] Wintz goes on to say, "From the moment that this concept originated around the turn of the century there were conflicting interpretations about precisely what the term meant."[6] The visualization of these definitions, which ranged from a commitment to self-help to Pan-Africanist ideals, were found in some of the photographs of the period. The images depicted people proud of their race, self-reliant and insistent upon their rights as full citizens.

The photographs made during this period on the Hampton campus exemplify pride and determination. They also reflect and represent the dreams and ideals of the black working class. In reading the photographs of Johnston's Hampton, one perceives a sense of well-being and a feeling that the future of African Americans will be productive, healthy, and spiritually sound. Hampton through the lens of Johnston is a conundrum. As Judith Fryer Davidov wrote, "Stillness predominates. Although the purpose of the

Hampton Institute—as a number of 'before' and 'after' shots make clear—was to transform the primitive, squalid, and disorderly into the improved, well kept, and civilized, the absolute containment of these photographs is in itself tantalizing, perhaps because it belies what we viewers today know: that these images of inviolate tranquility at Hampton are not in fact the 'after,' but scenes of utopian perfection, moments of arrest."[7] This was a radical notion considering that many of Johnston's photographs were created within sixty years of the abolition of slavery.

Johnston's ability to approach her subjects in a variety of ways gives us a broader picture of the students in this community. Johnston's photographs explored the lives of the educated and the poor residing near the institute, allowing the contemporary reader to analyze these experiences within the realm of a privileged eye and a segregated American culture. Her well-orchestrated images of life on the college campus create a protected and idealized image. These photographs took on the responsibility of informing and constructing the image of black life guided by Hampton founder General Samuel Chapman Armstrong's edict "to teach Negroes to become better workers, not political activists . . . to make of them not accomplished scholars, but to build up character and manhood. . . . Male students, required to wear uniforms, were organized into a cadet corps that march to classes and meals; each student and his room were inspected daily. Women students were closely supervised by teachers and dormitory matrons . . . taught to cook and sew, to set a proper table, to acquire all the graces that would make a good housewife—or housekeeper."[8]

Johnston presented both the black elite and the working poor, focusing on racist theories and the resulting effects of racism. Finally, the images served many opposing positions: while reinforcing white hegemony they celebrated the lives of the young men and women whose families sought to create a new social status in American culture, along with a new visual identity as the New Negro for a New Century.

—DEBORAH WILLIS-KENNEDY
*Director of Exhibitions, Anacostia Museum
and Center for African-American History and Culture,
Smithsonian Institution*

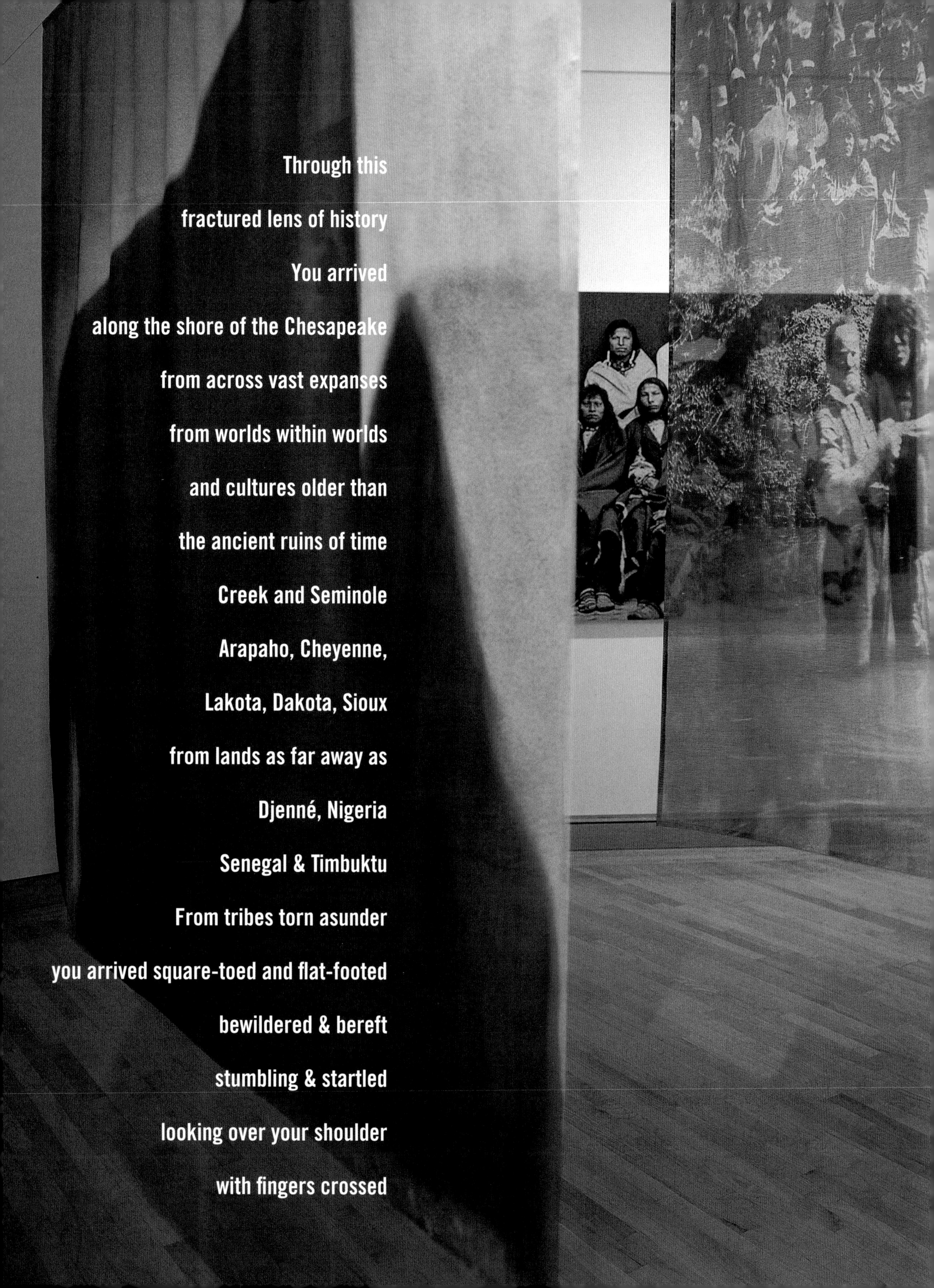

Through this

fractured lens of history

You arrived

along the shore of the Chesapeake

from across vast expanses

from worlds within worlds

and cultures older than

the ancient ruins of time

Creek and Seminole

Arapaho, Cheyenne,

Lakota, Dakota, Sioux

from lands as far away as

Djenné, Nigeria

Senegal & Timbuktu

From tribes torn asunder

you arrived square-toed and flat-footed

bewildered & bereft

stumbling & startled

looking over your shoulder

with fingers crossed

At Hampton you arrived

as prisoners of war & freed-slaves

You arrived and

displaced & dislocated

acquiring the ways of the patriarch

Leaving blankets and chains at the door

became your practice

you checked in one way

assuming its name

and came out another

your fate, your progress now measured

but your Missionary instruction

by your successful distance

would *not* be

from your past

to Conserve a Legacy

God and education

had posed as the perfect package deal

& your soul was the price of the ticket

Educated away from yourself

you gave up Ogun, Ife, Yemoja,

Obatala & Wankan alike

for a single and alien god

Ashe floating by on a red cloud

A VIEW FROM
HAMPTON UNIVERSITY MUSEUM

During the 1899–1900 academic year, when Hampton Normal and Agricultural Institute commissioned the noted photographer Frances Benjamin Johnston to do a series of photographs documenting the work of the school, Hampton had about one thousand students. According to Principal Hollis Burke Frissell, of that number about four hundred were children from the "neighborhood." Most of the other students were from Virginia, but more than twenty states were represented in the student body, which included 135 Native American students.

Students had several options depending on their preparation, interests, and gender. They could pursue studies in the Academic Department, in the Post-Graduate Course, in the Trade School if the student was male, or the Domestic Science Department if female. Every student had regular instruction in agriculture; land ownership and self-sufficiency were early and consistent goals for Hampton students.

When General Samuel Chapman Armstrong founded Hampton in 1868, his primary goal was to train teachers who would return to their rural southern communities to found and staff schools for the advancement of African-Americans. As the school's scope expanded in 1878 to incorporate American Indians, the mission of creating "teachers and leaders" was extended to native students who would return to their tribal communities. For these reasons, Frissell reported in 1900 that "The great majority of Hampton's 1,031 graduates and many of its undergraduates are or have been teaching in the free schools of Virginia and other states. They have taught since 1868 more than 130,000 children in eighteen states in the South and the West." Frissell wrote, "the work of the school never seemed better worth doing or more hopeful than at present."

Over the course of the twentieth century, Hampton developed from a secondary school into a four-year college in 1930, and then in 1984 into a university. In 1999, when Carrie Mae Weems visited the Hampton University campus to do research for the Williams College Museum of Art commission, Hampton was well into its greatest period of change, growth, and transition. Over the previous two

decades, the university had doubled in size, the student body growing to 5,824 students drawn from fifty-nine states, territories, and foreign countries. Numerous academic programs had been added, standards for students raised, research increased, campus facilities enhanced, cultural and athletic opportunities expanded, and community development partnerships created. One hundred years after Johnston had created her *Hampton Album*, the university defined itself as "a comprehensive institution of higher education, dedicated to the promotion of learning through outstanding teaching, research, scholarship, and service. Its curricular emphases are scientific and professional, with a strong liberal arts undergirding."

In 1996, when the Hampton University Museum first agreed to collaborate with the Williams College Museum of Art on a project, it was described as a two-part exhibition focused on Frances Benjamin Johnston's *Hampton Album* of 1900. The first part would present a selection of Johnston's work; the second would be the work of a contemporary African American or American Indian female photographer responding to the Johnston photographs and to life at Hampton today. The Williams College Museum of Art chose Carrie Mae Weems as that photographer. Our suggestion that an American Indian photographer be included as well, because of Hampton's history and the fact that the current student body includes people of both heritages, was rejected.

Over its four-year incubation period, the exhibition's focus changed several times. In May 1997, Carrie Mae Weems paid a brief visit to the campus, her first. Two years later, in the spring of 1999, she returned and with the assistance of museum and archives staff had numerous images from the archival collection scanned. After her second visit, the artist decided to include materials related to Hampton's historic American Indian education program (1878–1923). Hampton learned of this change in plans in late September, and the description of what she was planning caused considerable concern.

Strong objection was expressed to Weems's idea of appropriating, for her part of the exhibition, the names from headstones in the school's cemetery of Native American students. The approach she proposed was in direct opposition to the efforts, ongoing for well over a decade at Hampton, to break down stereotypes, to treat contemporary and historical people as individuals with unique stories, and above all, to have them speak for themselves about their lives. Weems proposed to draw parallels between the experience of Hampton's African American and American Indian students. Our position was that while her good intentions were not in question, she simply did not have a strong enough understanding of the facts to address these issues meaningfully. To her credit, Weems withdrew her proposal.

In an attempt to more fully explain our profound reservations about the direction of the project, materials on stereotyping, on perspectives of appropriating culture and history for other purposes, on the history of some Native American and African American students who attended Hampton, and on the issue of boarding schools in American Indian history were gathered and sent to the artist. These materials were selected to reveal the complexities of the issues, the sensitivities involved in interpreting this history, and most specifically, to reinforce the importance of not placing all Hampton African American students and all Hampton American Indian students in homogeneous groups so as to make generalizations about them.

Incorporated in *Carrie Mae Weems: The Hampton Project* are thirteen images created over more than half a century at Hampton. Weems said at her talk at the exibition opening that "education is conformity," and that is the larger message of her work. This message is questionable at best in that many people have been moved to rebellion by access to education. Frederick Douglass talked about education as liberation. However, the more objectionable part of Weems's work is not its dubious message, but that the artist appropriated images of real people who had/have real lives and real stories, and decreed meaning that may or may not fit the facts of these individual lives. At the Hampton University Museum the effort is to diligently strive never to portray people as nameless victims. We try not to assume or to convey that all Native American students or all African American students have the same experience, same goals, same beliefs, and same reactions to historical forces. We do try to present history and culture from the perspective and in the voice of those who have lived it. Because we feel the exhibition concept is incompatible with Hampton's approach to using historical information and cultural materials, the exhibition will not travel to the Hampton University Museum.

Perhaps those who see this exhibition and do not know the history of Hampton University or are not familiar with the historical photographs of Hampton will find something useful and provocative in *Carrie Mae Weems: The Hampton Project.* But others will see a turn-of-the-century photograph of Frank Dean Banks, Hampton class of 1876, at home with his family having dinner. Banks was employed by Hampton from 1877 to 1923. When the photograph was taken in 1899–1900 he was head bookkeeper in the Treasurer's Office. His son, Leonard, a 1908 graduate of Hampton, also served as a bookkeeper in the Treasurer's Office for more than a year before going on to study dentistry. At the end of his career, he served as the Hampton Institute dentist. Or they will see Louis Firetail (Sioux, Crow Creek) photographed that same year wearing tribal clothing, standing in front of Jane Worcester's class in American history. Or they will see D. R. Lewis's mechanical drawing class, also photographed in 1899–1900. Some people may even recognize their classmates or themselves in the more recent photographs Weems used.

One of the photographs that Weems uses is a page from the 1934 Hampton yearbook, with graduates' photographs laid out in the shape of an H. The class of 1934 at Hampton was a particularly distinguished one. Graduates that year went on to become presidents of three colleges; a president of the United Negro College Fund; the founder and head of a major publishing organization; a Hampton University professor emeritus, who also continues to be the only person to have chaired both the Virginia Commission for the Arts and the Virginia Foundation for Humanities and Public Policy; and the founder of the first native college of music in South Africa, also recognized as one of the country's premier composers of the twentieth century. Several members of that class and their families still live in the Hampton community. Most of them have devoted their lives to education. They deserve more than to see themselves, their classmates, or their family members included anonymously in an exhibition that to our mind simplifies education and the struggle to attain it as "conformity."

—JEANNE ZEIDLER
Director, Hampton University Museum

INTERVIEW: *Carrie Mae Weems*

Denise Ramzy: How is the making of your work affected or influenced by your sense of the audience?

Carrie Mae Weems: I don't make work based on what I think people want to hear or see. If I did, *The Hampton Project* would be a very different work. Critical practice is central to my way of working, and is an important aspect in all my work, including "Family Pictures and Stories." [*Laughs*] In my work, even I don't get off the hook.

So from this vantage point, I produce work that is essential to our cultural dialogue; work that opens the door to critical discussion, debate, and dialogue; work that needs to be made. Of course, some audiences will be alienated by my work and by my intention, Hampton University being a case in point, but it's a risk worth taking.

Katherine Fogg: Can you talk a bit about your process? How did you begin?

CMW: I found out about Hampton University through Frances B. Johnston's *Hampton Album.* Isn't that fabulous—the work of Johnston introducing Carrie Mae Weems to a Black university! God works in mysterious ways. So I visited Hampton on one of my many sojourns to the South. At any rate, I started *The Hampton Project* by making several visits. Three years ago I had no idea how the piece might take shape; however, I start every project by reading and by looking around in an attempt to develop a sense of the place. I made and collected photographs, interviewed students, and visited the campus. Basically, I built my own personal archive of selected materials.

I also did a bit of reading on the nature of democracy, turning my attention to the greatest Virginian of them all—Thomas Jefferson—in order to better understand the significant opinions that continue to shape our notions of democracy, assimilation, and education. It's much too involved to discuss here, suffice it to say that the new Republic demanded conformity, consistency of opinion, manner, and mores. Democracy does not tolerate dissent and/or difference; by its very nature it demands conformity; a republic of like-minded men and women is essential to the democratic process. Those who refused to submit were driven to the stony wall, the edge of time, the buffalo jump, thus the separate fate of blacks and Indians.

Now, I'm usually interested in little-known facts about a place. It's often the little-known facts and secrets that make a place/thing/person; the little things illuminate and reveal the essence of a thing; they provide the shape and character. God is in the details, or "in the particularity of difference," as [film maker and cultural critic] Trinh T. Minh-ha would say.

Hampton University is unique for several reasons: it's the first educational institution in North America to offer programs of study to both African Americans and North American Indians; it has a tremendous archive that includes thousands of photographs—many of Indians on the central plains—along with a rather impressive collection of tribal artifacts, including a number of student donations; and several Hampton students became missionaries, both in Africa and on Indian lands, returning among their people to work, to convert. In 1868 its first students were freed slaves, and in 1878 its first Indian students were former hostages and prisoners of war—a fascinating contradiction; it is considered by many to be the black Harvard of the South; and finally, buried in its university cemetery are thirty-eight Native Americans (I refer to twenty-three of them in the audio), which is contrary to Native American spiritual beliefs. A gold mine and a land mine.

Now, to my mind, these specific features make Hampton a treasure trove and a perfect site for beginning a critical dialogue that focuses on the problematic nature of assimilation, identity, and the role of education. Don't get me wrong, education has its advantages; and the fact that black Americans in leadership positions historically have come from southern black institutions is extremely important. This is a given, but personally I'm interested in the tangled web of history, in the rough edges, and the bumpy surface, the mess just beneath the veneer of order.

KF: And how did *The Hampton Project* change over time and become what it is now?

CMW: The turning point in my conceptual thinking about the project came after a marvelous meeting with Hampton honor students—for this I have Jeanne Zeidler to thank. I asked the students what they considered most important about Hampton, and what they would want others to know about the place. Several ideas were tossed about and discussed, someone spoke eloquently about "The Head, the Hand, and the Heart," but finally a very articulate female student said: "You know, I walk through this campus often. I love this campus on the shore of the Chesapeake, but one day I noticed the street names, and I realized for the first time—truly realized—that they were Indian names; and it occurred to me that at one time Native Americans [helped build] this school so that I could go to school. And I think that's something that people should know. It's important."

So the decision about how to approach the piece was really made with valuable input from Hampton students. This is why I'm so disappointed that the Hampton venue was cancelled. I knew that a critical approach would make the museum administration somewhat uncomfortable, but I also felt that a poetic and critical probing of the more complex issues surrounding Hampton's history would be essential to the project. Nothing moves forward without sincerely looking at the multiple levels of reality, and unbridled reality is often painful, if you know what I mean. But one learns from looking, from seeing, and by not hiding from the revealing aspects of the truth.

KF: How did you decide to use the banners and the audio?

CMW: I prefer the word photograph to banner; at any rate, I've been tired of walls for a long time and much more interested in developing a certain kind of physicality for both myself and my audience. I wanted to play with the idea of suspension; for instance, suspension of belief, time, and space. So I began suspending materials from the ceiling. I used cloth banners for the first time in "And 22 Million Very Tired and Very Angry People;" in that installation the text banners acted as flowing signifiers. In this installation [of *The Hampton Project*] the pictures are printed on sheer, diaphanous cloth, which allows for the creation of many semitransparent layers, each image therefore building up on the next and each acquiring new meanings based on the particular way the photographs are situated, one to the other. It's been a very exciting way of working.

By moving into and through the work, I wanted to give the viewer permission to invade the work of art, to invade history, and thereby claim it as one's own; to feel that one is a part of history and, therefore, one makes history. In this way, the viewer is transformed from audience to participant/observer.

Again, I'm interested in a certain kind of physicalness, and I've often thought about how to move people from point A to point B, my feeling being that if you can move through the work, you can move through the experience, the experience then becomes not mine, but ours.

Of course, I'm particularly intrigued by sound, music, rhythm, and language, and have used audio in a number of pieces. The voice is an instrument, and I try to be aware of this fact and use it. In my texts the words function as lyrics, and the speaker as singer. The presence of audio allows me to control the mood of the space and the pace of movement in the space. Invariably, people slow down the minute they enter the installation space; and in part this has to do with the nature of soothing sound, it makes you listen. So the images and the sound take on a contemplative quality that I personally find very appealing.

KF: You incorporate yourself in the image of the buffalo falling off the cliff.

CMW: Yes, the David Wojnarowicz piece is in the background. I wanted to pay homage to him. I often include myself in my work, it has to do with wanting to inscribe my presence in the things that I consider important. I also insert myself as the narrator of history. Women are the weepers of history, we are the symbolic representations of compassion and decency. I find this representation useful and I use it as a vehicle in my work.

DR: Which brings me to Frances B. Johnston; how do you see your installation in concert with her *Hampton Album*?

CMW: It's the perfect juxtaposition. Of course, there is the obvious difference. [*Smiles*] As artists what we make has a lot to do with the time in which we live. Frances worked at the beginning of this century and produced the *Hampton Album* primarily to raise much needed money for the school, and I respect Johnston's work and her commitment very much. I'm working at the end of the century and so have other concerns, concerns about the very nature of representation, about who makes and who looks, who decides, etc. These are contemporary concerns of a critical nature, and they are questions that allow me to be profoundly engaged with both the past and the future. With this in mind, I make photographs for a different reason and function.

Form follows content. So I make 'em, find 'em, scan 'em, clip 'em, you know, all that stuff that modern computer technology allows me to do, I do.

KF: There is a ghostly quality about *The Hampton Project*, there's something very mystical about it. Can you talk about that?

CMW: Ghosts are my company, they speak to me and tell me what to say. But perhaps what you sense is the spirit of justice the work seeks. I fight for what I believe to be right; this is my spiritual challenge, always and in every way to embrace the breadth of our humanity, it's my duty to myself and the way that I am responsible to you; and this is so, even when it hurts.

DR: Do you think your earlier work is relevant to *The Hampton Project*?

CMW: Of course. First off, all of my projects refer to the critical role of representation, both socially and in the work of art. That said, besides making work I consider to be formally engaging, my interest lies in moving folks from the margins to the center by employing various representational strategies that allow representations of people of color to stand for the human multitudes, more than as degraded symbols for blackness.

To backtrack for a moment, getting off the wall and hanging objects in space meant that regardless of the viewer's ethnicity, the viewer has to pass through multiple layers of identity, experience, etc. Being in it and of it offers the possibility of changing perception. An "I am you and you are me" kind of thing. It's a little more complex, but you get my drift.

The question that I grapple with is how to change my perceptions, and impact yours. So I insist that my subjects

of colored peoples can and must stand for humanity. My little manifesto, credo, ditto.

DR: When you chose to focus on Native Americans for *The Hampton Project*, did it occur to you that one way to get that point across was to represent Native Americans along side African Americans?

CMW: Absolutely. The assumption is that I'm black and therefore should, could, would, deal with only the obvious subject areas. You know, stay in my place, my space. This kind of thinking is epidemic, rampant. I'm black and Native American, but I don't know any more about being Indian than I know about being African, such is my fate, my raw deal, the bum wrap. At this point it no longer matters. What matters is that I assume that I have the right to speak about any- and everything affecting you, me, us, and them. I assume that I can speak from multiple places and in multiple contexts. And even if I'm wrong, I assume that I can speak for those who can't or are too afraid to speak up for themselves. I have a very big mouth and opinions on just about everything.

Check this out, often reviewers reduce "Untitled (Kitchen Table Series)" to the woes of black men and women. Cut and dried. But the piece is loaded, carrying serious baggage, and I'm trying to unpack it all—i.e., the politics of gender, identity, desire, etc.—as well as trying to locate new representational roles for women, as object, subject, and maker. The work was essential to my own process in deconstructing history and photography and the object/subject divide. Loaded. In "Untitled (Kitchen Table Series)" woman takes charge of her image, controls it, plays it and likes it, looks back and loves it. It's not "I am woman, I am strong" nonsense, it's about a certain level of consciousness. "Sometimes you feel like a nut, sometimes you don't."

Am I only important because I'm an African American artist? Poor thing! I would really hate to think so. I've always thought that my presence enhances any gathering.

This interview between the artist and Katherine Fogg and Denise Ramzy, both Williams College class of 2000, took place in April and May 2000 during Weems's residency at Williams College.

FROM A GREAT HEIGHT I SAW YOU FALLING
BLACK AND INDIAN ALIKE
AND FOR YOU SHE PLAYED
A SORROW SONG

With your
your extended
reaching
up and

Alpha, Omega, Delta, Psi

I saw you
but yet & still
become Hampton Alums
survival's people
the graduates of a stripped people
Still numb from the shock
echoes of your former selves
I saw your dissipating fear
hollowed relics
and watched you emerge
of a former time

I saw you

Black and Indian co-mingle
I saw you challenging
building the structure
the institution &
of your survival
demanding more than
brick by brick
reserved land
with your own hands
peanuts and twenty acres & a mule
in your own time
Against the wind
From ash and dust and twilight
I saw your quest for more
I saw you clawing and rising
and saw you smile
inch by inch & side by side
at the sweet smell of success
and then sadly move along

parallel lines

VIRGINIA MEDICINE-BULL

ARMSTRONG FIRE-CLOUD

LOUISA BANKS

ELIZABETH KENNEDY

SIMON MAZAKUTE

JOSEPH TASUNKA-WASTE

And against the odds

ENOCH CONKLIN SAVARPKS

I saw you become many things you

BENJAMIN BEAR-BIRD

were not supposed to be

MAHPIYA-MANI

and to my horror I saw

OLIVE MADISON

some of you die trying

GEORGE NORCROSS HIPOYA

For those of you

EDITH YELLOW-HAIR

whose remains

FRANCIS RENCONTRE

remain here

LORA BOWED-HEAD SNOW

the ancestors are still weeping and

MARY TURNER

calling out your names

NICK PRATT

THOMAS NOBLE

JOHN BLUE-PIPE

FRANCESCA RIOS

CRACKING-WING

MARY RED-BIRD

EVA GOOD-ROAD

MARY PRETTY-HAIR

BIOGRAPHY AND SELECTED BIBLIOGRAPHY

CARRIE MAE WEEMS

Biography
Born in Portland, Oregon, 1953

Education
B.F.A., California Institute of the Arts,
   Valencia, 1981
M.F.A., University of California, San Diego, 1984
Graduate Program in Folklore, University of California,
   Berkeley, 1984–87
Honorary Doctorate, California College of Arts
   and Crafts, Oakland, 1999

Teaching Experience
Teaching Assistant, University of California,
   San Diego, 1983–84
Teacher, San Diego City College, 1984
Teaching Assistant,
   University of California, Berkeley, 1987
Assistant Professor, Hampshire College,
   Amherst, Massachusetts, 1987–91
Visiting Professor, Hunter College, New York,
   New York, 1988–89
Assistant Professor, California College of the Arts and
   Crafts, Oakland, 1991
Sterling A. Brown, Class of 1922, Visiting Professor,
   Williams College, Williamstown,
   Massachusetts, 2000
Resident Artist, Skowhegan School of Painting
   and Sculpture, summer 2000

Awards, Grants, and Residencies
Los Angeles Women's Building Poster Award, 1981
University of California Fellowship Award, 1981–85
University of California Chancellor's Grant, 1982
California Arts Council Grant, 1983

Artist in Residence, Visual Studies
   Workshop, Rochester, New York, 1986
Smithsonian Fellow, Smithsonian Institution,
   Washington, D.C., 1987
Massachusetts Artists Fellowship (finalist), 1988
Artist in Residence, Light Work, Syracuse,
   New York, 1988
Massachusetts Artists Fellowship (finalist), 1989
Massachusetts Artists Fellowship (finalist), 1990
Artist in Residence, Rhode Island School of
   Design, Providence, 1989–90
Artist in Residence, Art Institute of Chicago, 1990
Artist in Residence, The Fabric Workshop/Museum,
   Philadelphia, 1991–93
Louis Comfort Tiffany Award, 1992
Artist in Residence, Cité des Arts, Paris, 1993–94
National Endowment for the Arts Visual Arts Grant,
   1994–95
The Alpert Award for Visual Arts, 1996
Artist in Residence, Künstlerhaus Bethanien, Berlin,
   1997–98

Commissions
Percent for Art, City of New York, 1994–99
Liz Claiborne, Domestic Violence,
   Programs in Public Art, 1995
J. Paul Getty Museum, *From Here I Saw What
   Happened and I Cried*, 1995
Chicago Public Library, City of Chicago, 1996
47th Venice Biennale, *Framed by Modernism
   (Portrait of Robert Colescott)*, 1997
New York State Public Arts Program, Walden School,
   Bronx, *The Spirit of Mind, Body, and Health*, 1999
Santa Barbara Museum of Art, *The Jefferson Suites*, 1999
Williams College Museum of Art,
   The Hampton Project, 2000

BIBLIOGRAPHY

Aletti, Vince. "Choices." *The Village Voice* (October 30, 1990): 105.

_____. "Dark Passage." *The Village Voice* (December 22, 1992): 102–03.

_____. "Review." *The Village Voice* (November 14, 1995).

Anderson, Michael. "Review." *Art Issues* (Summer 1995): 42.

The Art of Advocacy. Ridgefield, Connecticut: Aldrich Museum, 1991.

Barnard, Elissa. "American Activist Art: No Laughing Matter." *Mail Star* (March 6, 1992): C8.

Behr, Martin. "Ist Rassismus ein Sehfehler? Mit Fotos auf Identitätssuche." *Salzburger Nachrichten* (May 7, 1993).

Benner, Susan. "A Conversation with Carrie Mae Weems." *Art Week 23* (May 7, 1992): 4–5.

Bonetti, David. "Looking Truth in the Face. Carrie Mae Weems Delivers Political Messages with Human Spirit." *San Francisco Examiner* (June 18, 1993): E7.

_____. "A Question of Colors." *San Francisco Examiner* (June 6, 1993).

_____. "Visual History of African America." *San Francisco Examiner* (May 9, 1995): C3.

Braff, Phyllis. "How Artists' Creations Relate to Society." *The New York Times* (May 2, 1993).

Bricker Balken, Debra. "Review." *Art in America* (April 1992): 129–30.

Burning Issues: Contemporary African-American Art. Fort Lauderdale, Florida: Museum of Art, 1996.

Canning, Susan. "Review." *Art Papers 20* (March/April 1996): 50.

Carrie Mae Weems. Philadelphia: Fabric Workshop/Museum, in conjunction with 10th Dakar Biennale, 1996.

Carrie Mae Weems: Ritual & Revolution. Berlin: Künstlerhaus Bethanien, 1998.

"Carrie Mae Weems/Matrix 115, Wadsworth Athenaeum." *Journal of the Print World* (Spring 1991): 49.

"Carrie Mae Weems to Create Installation Exploring Representation of African Americans in Photography." *Los Angeles Bay News* (February 23, 1995).

Coleman, A. D. "Cultural Tenacity Among the Gullah." *The New York Observer* (December 21, 1992): 14.

Curtis, Cathy. "Down-Home Look Belies Power of Carrie Mae Weems's Work." *Los Angeles Times* (October 21, 1991): F3.

Dartnall, Collette. "Invisibility Black Identity in the Work of Carrie Mae Weems and Lorna Simpson." Master's thesis, University of Southern California, 1997.

Dislocations. Finland: Rovaniemi Art Museum/Harper Collins Publishers, 1997.

"Disputed Identities." *San Francisco Camerawork 17*, no. 3 (Fall 1990).

Doniger, Sidney, Sandra Matthews, and Gilllian Brown, eds. "Personal Perspectives on the Evolution of American Black Photography." *Obscura 2.* no. 4 (Spring 1982): 8–17.

Dowd, Maureen. "Yes, But Can She Make Them Swoon." *The New York Times* (May 26, 1991): E6.

Dubin, Zan. "Black and Wright." *Los Angeles Times* (October 10, 1991).

Felchin, Nina. *No Laughing Matter.* New York: Independent Curators Incorporated, 1991.

Foerstner, Abigail. "Take a Spring Stroll to Four River North Galleries." *Chicago Tribune* (April 30, 1993): sec. 7, p. 89.

Frank, Peter. "Art Picks of the Week: Carrie Mae Weems, Charles Gaines, Noah Purifoy." *L.A. Weekly* (June 9–15, 1995.)

Freeland, Cynthia. *The Other.* Houston: Houston Center for Photography, 1988.

Galassi, Peter. *The Pleasures and Terrors of Domestic Comfort.* New York: Museum of Modern Art, 1991.

_____. "Pleasures and Terrors of Domestic Comfort." *Papel Alpha 2* (1996): 20.

Gibbs, Michael. "Critical Realism." *Perspektief 39*, Rotterdam, The Netherlands (1990): 38–58.

"Goings On About Town." *The New Yorker* (May 25, 1992).

Golden, Thelma. *Black Male, Representations of Masculinity in Contemporary American Art.* New York: Whitney Museum of American Art/Harry N. Abrams, 1994.

Hagen, Charles. "Gullah Culture Casts Its Spell." *The New York Times* (November 1992): C1, C22.

Hall, Stuart. "Minimal Selves." *ICA Document 6*: Identity. London: ICA, 1987.

Halle, Howard. "Review." *Time Out New York* (January 24–31, 1996): 26.

Harper, Glenn, ed. *Interventions and Provocations: Conversations on Art, Culture, and Resistance.* Albany, New York: State University of New York Press, 1998.

Heartney, Eleanor. "Carrie Mae Weems." *ARTnews* (January 1991): 154–55.

_____. "Carrie Mae Weems at P.P.O.W." *ARTnews* (February 1993): 109.

Henry, Gerrit. "Books in Review." *Print Collector's Newsletter* (September/October, 1993): 109.

hooks, bell. "Talking Art with Carrie Mae Weems." *Art on My Mind: Visual Politics.* New York: The New Press, 1995.

"Interview." *Atelier*, Japan (January 1991): 35–37.

In These Islands: South Carolina, Georgia. Tuscaloosa, Alabama: Sarah Moody Gallery of Art, University of Alabama, 1994.

Jackson, Phyllis J. "(In)forming the Visual: (Re)presenting Women of African Descent." *International Review of African-American Art 14*, vol. 3 (1997): 31.

Johnson, Patricia C. "Balance at the Table." *Houston Chronicle* (April 8, 1996).

Jones, Kellie. "In Their Own Image." *Artforum 29*, no. 3 (November 1990): 133–38.

Joselit, David. "Exhibiting Gender." *Art in America* (January 1997): 36–39.

Kashara, Michiko. *The Politics Behind the Nude.* Tokyo: Chikuma Shobo Publishing Co., 1998.

Kasrel, Deni. "Engrossing Photo Exhibit at ICA." *Philadelphia Business Journal* (December 1994).

Kelley, Jeff. "The Isms Brothers: Carrie Mae Weems at SFAI." *Art Week 23* (May 7, 1992): 4.

Kimmelman, Michael. "Black Male." *The New York Times* (November 11, 1994).

_____. "When a Glint in the Eye Showed Crime in the Genes." *The New York Times* (May 22, 1998): E31.

Kirsh, Andrea, and Susan Fisher Sterling. *Carrie Mae Weems.* 1992. Rev. ed. Washington, DC: National Museum of Women in the Arts, 1994.

Lewis, Jo Ann. "Lessons in the Stories: The Engaging Voice of Carrie Mae Weems." *The Washington Post* (January 7, 1993): C2.

Linker, Kate. "Went Looking for Africa." *Artforum 31* (February 1993): 79–82.

Littlefield, Kinney. "Photography and Poetry Extract Beauty from Pain." *The Orange County Register* (October 25, 1991): 48.

MacDonald, Cathy. "Frighteningly Funny." *The Daily News,* Nova Scotia (March 5, 1992).

McCloud, Kathleen. "Twist and Turn of Truth." *Pasatiempo* (April 4, 1997): 42.

McKenna, Kristine. "The Evolution of a Tough Cookie." *Los Angeles Times* (June 27, 1993): 4.

Mellor, Carl. "No Joke: Photographer Carrie Mae Weems Blasts Away Stereotypes." *Syracuse New Times* (August 31–September 7, 1998): 1ff.

Miller-Keller, Andrea, and Judith Wilson. *Carrie Mae Weems/Matrix 115.* Hartford, Connecticut: Wadsworth Athenaeum, 1991.

Moore, Catronia. "The Art of Political Correctness." *Art & Text 41,* Melbourne, Australia (1992): 32–39.

Muchnic, Suzanne. "Going for a Gut Reaction." *Los Angeles Times* (February 26, 1995).

Original Visions, Shifting the Paradigm, Women's Art 1970–1996. Boston: McMullen Museum of Art, Boston College Office of Publications, 1997.

Patterson, Tom. "Photograph exhibit at SECCA focuses on African-American life." *Winston-Salem Journal* (December 19, 1993): C3.

Piché, Thomas, Jr., and Thelma Golden. *Carrie Mae Weems: Recent Work, 1992–1998.* New York: George

BLACK MAN WITH A WATERMELON

Black Man with Watermelon, from "Ain't Jokin," 1987-88

Nesbit, Perry. *Family Pictures and Stories: A Photographic Installation.* Reading, Pennsylvania: Freedman Gallery, Albright College Center for the Arts, 1991.

Neumaier, Diane. *Reframings: New American Feminist Photographies.* Philadelphia: Temple University Press, 1996.

1991 Biennial Exhibition. New York: Whitney Museum of American Art, 1991.

Braziller Publisher, in association with Everson Museum of Art, Syracuse, New York, 1998. (withdrawn from publication)

Plagens, Peter. "A House Is Not a Home." *Newsweek* (October 21, 1991): 62–63.

A Portrait Is Not a Likeness. Tucson: Center for Creative Photography, University of Arizona, 1991.

Powell, Richard J. *Black Art and Culture in the Twentieth Century.*

London: Thames and Hudson, 1997.

Princethal, Nancy. "Carrie Mae Weems at P.P.O.W." *Art in America* (January 1991): 129.

Reid, Calvin. "Carrie Mae Weems." *Arts Magazine 65,* no. 5 (January 1991).

Re/righting History: Counternarratives by Contemporary African-American Artists. Katonah, New York: Katonah Museum of Art, 1999.

Rich, Ruby. "Weems's World." *Mirabella* (February 1993): 44–45.

Richardson, Trevor. *Fictions of the Self: A Portrait of Contemporary Photography.* Greensboro, North Carolina: Weatherspoon Art Gallery, University of North Carolina at Greensboro; Amherst, Massachusetts: Herter Art Gallery, University of Massachusetts, 1993.

Roland, Marya. "Tragic Wake…." *Art Papers* (March/April 1997): 68.

Rosenthal, Mel. "Commentary." *Nueva Luz 2* (1989): 22–32.

Saunders, Charles. "No Laughing Matter." *The Daily News,* Sunday Perspective (April 12, 1992).

Schmerler, Sarah. "Review." *Time Out New York* (November 22–29, 1995): 25.

Schwarze Kunst Konzept zur Politik und Identität. Berlin: Neue Gesellschaft für Bildende Kunst, 1992.

Schwendenwein, Jude. "A Look at Privilege, Presumption." *The Hartford Courant* (November 18, 1990): G6.

Shaw, Thomas M. "Review." *African Arts* (April 1993): 81.

Sherlock, Maureen P. "A Dangerous Age: The Midlife Crisis of Postmodern Feminism." *Arts Magazine* 65, no. 1 (September 1990): 17–74.

Sichel, Berta. "Carrie Mae Weems retrata a disápora negra." *Terca-Feira*, São Paulo, Brazil (February 6, 1996): D8.

Siegel, Jeanne. "The 1991 Whitney Biennial." *Tema Celeste* (May/June 1991): 97.

Skvirshy, Karina, and Jennifer Pearson. *Art About Life: Contemporary American Culture.* Bloomington: Fine Arts Gallery, Indiana University, 1995.

Smith, Roberta. "A Photographer Upstages Herself." *The New York Times* (December 22, 1995).

Souter, Lucy. "By Any Means Necessary: Document and Fiction in the Work of Carrie Mae Weems." *Art & Design Profile*, no. 51 (1996): 70–75.

Sozanski, Edward. "An Emphatic View of History and Family." *The Philadelphia Inquirer* (December 9, 1994).

Squiers, Carol. "Domestic Blitz: The Modern Cleans House." *Artforum 30*, no. 2 (October 1991): 88–91.

Steinenger, Jutta. "Identitäten gegen die Klischees." *Kultur* (May 3, 1993).

Stevens, Mitchell. "A Family Affair." *New Art Examiner* (May 1992): 17.

Tamblyn, Christine. "Three Views of Families." *Artweek* (October 26, 1985): 11.

Tarlow, Lois. "Carrie Mae Weems." *Art New England* (August/ September 1991): 10–12.

Telling Histories: Installations by *Ellen Rothenberg and Carrie Mae Weems.* Seattle: University of Washington Press, 1999.

The Theater of Refusal: Black Art and Mainstream Criticism. Irvine: University of California, Irvine, Fine Arts Gallery, 1994.

Titz, Walter. "Schwarz, ich weiß, schwarz." *Kultur* (April 3, 1993).

Wallis, Brian. "Questioning Documentary." *Aperture 112* (Fall 1988): 60–71.

Wallis, Brian, ed. *Blasted Allegories: An Anthology of Writings by Contemporary Artists.* New York: New Museum of Contemporary Art; Cambridge: The MIT Press, 1988.

Watson, Stuart. "Critique." *Dalhousie News.* Halifax, Nova Scotia:

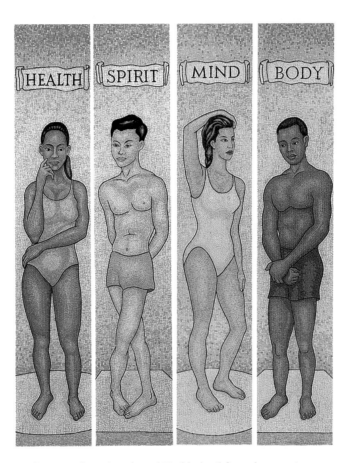

The Spirit of Mind, Body, and Health, detail from glass mosaic, 1999

Trippi, Laura. "And 22 Million Very Tired and Very Angry People." New York: New Museum of Contemporary Art, 1991.

Turner, Grady T. "Review." *Art in America* (June 1996): 103.

van Cook, Marguerite. "Carrie Mae Weems: The Right Questions." *Village Beat* (December 1990): 12.

Dalhousie University (April 8, 1992).

Weems, Carrie Mae. *And 22 Million Very Tired and Very Angry People.* San Francisco: Walter/ McBean Gallery, San Francisco Art Institute, 1992.

_____. *Blues & Pinks.* Artist's book, 1981.

_____. *Family Pictures and Stories: A Photographic Installation.* San Diego, California: Alternative Space Gallery, 1984.

_____. *THEN WHAT?* Photographs and Folklore. Buffalo, New York: CEPA Gallery, 1990.

_____. *Stories.* Artist's book, 1982

_____. *Vanishing Cream.* Artist's book, 1982.

Weibel, Peter. *Inclusion/Exclusion.* Austria: DuMont Bücheverlag, 1997.

Willis, Deborah, and Howard Dodson. *Black Photographers Bear Witness: 100 Years of Social Protest.* Williamstown, Massachusetts: Williams College Museum of Art, 1989.

Willis-Thomas, Deborah. *An Illustrated Bio-Bibliography of Black Photographers, 1940–1988.* New York: Garland Publishing, Inc., 1989.

Wilson, Judith. "Stereotypes, Or a Picture is Worth a Thousand Lies." *In Prisoners of Image: Ethnic and Gender Stereotypes.* New York: Alternative Museum, 1989.

Wise, Kelly. "Exhibit Spotlights Contemporary Artists." *The Boston Globe* (February 8, 1992): 16.

Wright, Erin. "Trustman House Exceptional Exhibit." *The Simmons News* (February 14, 1991): 8.

BIOGRAPHIES AND EXHIBITION CHECKLIST

CONSTANCE W. GLENN is Director of the University Art Museum at California State University—Long Beach. In addition to writing extensively on Frances Benjamin Johnston, she organized the traveling exhibition of Johnston's portrait works and co-authored the catalog *Frances Benjamin Johnston: Women of Class and Station*, (1979).

VIVIAN PATTERSON is Associate Curator, Collections Management at the Williams College Museum of Art and project manager for the exhibition *Carrie Mae Weems: The Hampton Project.* Her recent research has focused on the work of modernist artist Marguerite Zorach.

FREDERICK RUDOLPH is the Mark Hopkins Professor of History, Emeritus at Williams College. He is an authority on the history of Williams and has written extensively for professional journals in the fields of history and education. His publications include *Mark Hopkins and the Log: Williams College, 1836–1872* (1956); *The American College and University: A History* (1962); and *Curriculum: A History of the American Undergraduate Course of Study Since 1636* (1977).

KATHERINE FOGG and DENISE RAMZY are graduates of Williams College, Williamstown, Massachusetts, class of 2000. Under the supervision of Williams College Museum of Art director Linda Shearer and Hampton exhibition project manager Vivian Patterson, they conducted a series of interviews with Ms. Weems throughout spring 2000.

DEBORAH WILLIS-KENNEDY is curator of exhibitions at the Anacostia Museum for African-American Art and Culture at the Smithsonian Institution. Her most recent book, *Reflections in Black: A History of Black Photographers, 1840 to the Present*, accompanying the exhibition of the same name, appeared in summer 2000.

JEANNE ZEIDLER is director of the Hampton University Museum in Hampton, Virginia, and currently mayor of Williamsburg, Virginia. She has written extensively about Hampton University, its history, and her museum's expansive collections.

WILLIAMS COLLEGE MUSEUM OF ART EXHIBITION OF THE HAMPTON PROJECT, MARCH 4 –OCTOBER 22, 2000. IMAGES BY FRANCES BENJAMIN JOHNSTON, (AMERICAN, 1864–1952) FROM *THE HAMPTON ALBUM*:

Six of the Johnston works on display were vintage platinum prints from the Museum of Modern Art's Hampton Album, a gift from Lincoln Kirstein in 1965. The remaining nineteen images were derived from original prints in the Hampton University Archives. During the summer of 1999, while Hampton University's prints were at the Williamstown Art Conservation Center undergoing treatment and preparation for a traveling show, WCMA was granted permission to take them to Chicago Albumen Works in Housatonic, Massachusetts. where director Doug Munson made copy negatives of the images selected for the Williams exhibition. The platinum prints were made by Stephanie Ogeneski under Munson's direction in November and December 1999. The paper selected was 250gsm distaff white Crane's Cover, sized with alum and gelatin and hand-coated with platinum. The sheet size of the modern platinum prints is 8 7/16 inches high by 11 inches wide; the image size is 7 11/16 inches high by 9 11/16 inches wide. Each platinum copy print bears a blind stamp in the lower right-hand corner of the image with the initials CAW and the date 1999.

The Saw Mill: From Raft to Saw, ca. 1900/1999. Modern platinum print (copy negative derived from vintage platinum print); Image: 7 11/16"-by-9 11/16"; Sheet: 8 7/16"-by-11". Courtesy of the Collection of the Hampton University Archives, Hampton, Virginia.

Agriculture: Plant Life. Experiments with Plants and Soil, ca. 1900/1999. Modern platinum print (copy negative derived from vintage platinum print). Image: 7 11/16"-by-9 11/16"; Sheet: 8 7/16"-by-11". Courtesy of the Collection of the Hampton University Archives, Hampton, Virginia.

Stairway to the Treasurer's Residence: Students at Work, 1899-1900. Platinum print; Image: 7 9/16"-by-9 11/16"; Frame: 14 7/8"-by-18 7/8"-by-1 7/8". The Museum of Modern Art, New York. Gift of Lincoln Kirstein.

A Football Team, 1899-1900. Platinum print; Image: 7 9/16"-by-9 11/16"; Frame: 14 7/8"-by-18 7/8"-by-1 7/8". The Museum of Modern Art, New York. Gift of Lincoln Kirstein.

Physics: Estimating the Combined Draught of Horses, 1899-1900. Platinum print; Image: 7 5/8"-by-9 9/16"; Frame: 14 7/8"-by-18 7/8"-by-1 7/8". The Museum of Modern Art, New York. Gift of Lincoln Kirstein.

Geography: A Class in Current Events, 1899-1900. Platinum print; Image: 7 9/16"-by-9 11/16"; ; Frame: 14 7/8"-by-18 7/8"-by-1 7/8". The Museum of Modern Art, New York. Gift of Lincoln Kirstein.

Arithmetic: Measuring and Pacing, 1899–1900. Platinum print; Image: 7 9/16"-by-9 11/16"; Frame: 14 7/8"-by-18 7/8"-by-1 7/8". The Museum of Modern Art, New York. Gift of Lincoln Kirstein.

History: A Class in American History, 1899–1900. Platinum print; Image: 7 9/16"-by-9 11/16"; Frame: 14 7/8"-by-18 7/8"-by-1 7/8". The Museum of Modern Art, New York. Gift of Lincoln Kirstein.

A Guitar and Mandolin Club, ca. 1900/1999. Modern platinum print (copy negative derived from vintage platinum print); Image: 7 11/16"-by-9 5/8"; Sheet: 8 3/8"-by-11". Courtesy of the Collection of the Hampton University Archives, Hampton, Virginia.

A Lesson in Painting, ca. 1900/1999. Modern platinum print (copy negative derived from vintage platinum print); Image: 7 11/16"-by-9 11/16"; Sheet 8 7/16"-by-11". Courtesy of the Collection of the Hampton University Archives, Hampton, Virginia.

Trade School: Brick-laying, ca. 1900/1999. Modern platinum print (copy negative derived from vintage platinum print); Image: 7 11/16"-by-9 11/16"; Sheet 8 7/16"-by-11". Courtesy of the Collection of the Hampton University Archives, Hampton, Virginia.

Agriculture: Butter Making, ca. 1900/1999. Modern platinum print (copy negative derived from vintage platinum print); Image: 7 11/16"-by-9 11/16"; Sheet: 8 3/8"-by-11". Courtesy of the Collection of the Hampton University Archives, Hampton, Virginia.

Agriculture: Sampling Milk, ca. 1900/1999. Modern platinum print (copy negative derived from vintage platinum print); Image: 7 11/16"-by-9 11/16"; Sheet 8 7/16"-by-11". Courtesy of the Collection of the Hampton University Archives, Hampton, Virginia.

Agriculture: Judging a Dairy Cow, ca. 1900/1999. Modern platinum print (copy negative derived from vintage platinum print); Image: 7 11/16"-by-9 11/16"; Sheet 8 7/16"-by-11". Courtesy of the Collection of the Hampton University Archives, Hampton, Virginia.

Agriculture: Filling a Silo by Hand, ca. 1900/1999. Modern platinum print (copy negative derived from vintage platinum print); Image: 7 11/16"-by-9 11/16"; Sheet 8 7/16"-by-11". Courtesy of the Collection of the Hampton University Archives, Hampton, Virginia.

Agriculture: Mixing Fertilizer, ca. 1900/1999. Modern platinum print (copy negative derived from vintage platinum print); Image: 7 11/16"-by-9 5/8"; Sheet: 8 7/16"-by-11". Courtesy of the Collection of the Hampton University Archives, Hampton, Virginia.

Agriculture: Studying Soils at the Beach, or Formation of Soil by Active

Water, ca. 1900/1999. Modern platinum print (copy negative derived from vintage platinum print); Image: 7 11/16"-by-9 11/16"; Sheet: 8 3/8"-by-11". Courtesy of the Collection of the Hampton University Archives, Hampton, Virginia.

A Class in Dress-making, ca. 1900/1999. Modern platinum print (copy negative derived from vintage platinum print); Image: 7 11/16"-by-9 11/16"; Sheet: 8 3/8"-by-10 7/8". Courtesy of the Collection of the Hampton University Archives, Hampton, Virginia.

Gymnastics Class: Playing Basketball, ca. 1900/1999. Modern platinum print (copy negative derived from vintage platinum print) Image: 7 11/16"-by-9 5/8"; Sheet: 8 7/16"-by-11". Courtesy of the Collection of the Hampton University Archives, Hampton, Virginia.

Company Having Wand Drill, ca. 1900/1999. Modern platinum print (copy negative derived from vintage platinum print); Image: 7 11/16"-by-9 11/16"; Sheet: 8 7/16"-by-11". Courtesy of the Collection of the Hampton University Archives, Hampton, Virginia.

A Sketch Class at Work, ca. 1900/1999. Modern platinum print (copy negative derived from vintage platinum print); Image: 7 11/16"-by-9 11/16"; Sheet: 8 7/16"-by-11". Courtesy of the Collection of the Hampton University Archives, Hampton, Virginia.

Geography: Lesson on Local Industries—Lumber and Coal at the School Wharf, ca. 1900/1999. Modern platinum print (copy negative derived from vintage platinum print); Image: 7 11/16"-by-9 11/16"; Sheet: 8 7/16"-by-11". Courtesy of the Collection of the Hampton University Archives, Hampton, Virginia.

History: A Class at Fort Monroe, ca. 1900/1999. Modern platinum print (copy negative derived from vintage platinum print); Image: 7 11/16"-by-9 11/16"; Sheet: 8 7/16"-by-11". Courtesy of the Collection of the Hampton University Archives, Hampton, Virginia.

English Literature: Lesson on Whittier (Middle Class), ca. 1900/1999. Modern platinum print (copy negative derived from vintage platinum print); Image: 7 11/16"-by-9 11/16"; Sheet: 8 7/16"-by-11". Courtesy of the Collection of the Hampton University Archives, Hampton, Virginia.

Thanksgiving Day Lesson at Whittier, ca. 1900/1999. Modern platinum print (copy negative derived from vintage platinum print); Image: 7 11/16"-by-9 11/16"; Sheet: 8 7/16"-by-11". Courtesy of the Collection of the Hampton University Archives, Hampton, Virginia.

Saluting the Flag at Whittier Primary School, ca. 1900/1999. Modern platinum print (copy negative derived from vintage platinum print); Image: 7 11/16"-by-9 5/8"; Sheet: 8 7/16"-by-11". Courtesy of the Collection of the Hampton University Archives, Hampton, Virginia.

Memorial Church and Academic Hall: The Domestic Science Building Between Them, ca. 1900/1999. Modern platinum print (copy negative derived from vintage platinum print); Image: 7 11/16"-by-9 11/16"; Sheet: 8 7/16"-by-11". Courtesy of the Collection of the Hampton University Archives, Hampton, Virginia.

IMAGES BY CARRIE MAE WEEMS, ALL FROM *THE HAMPTON PROJECT*, 2000, AND COLLECTION OF THE ARTIST AND P.P.O.W.:

Cotton Picking. Ink on muslin banner; 96"-by-76" (p. 51)

Detail from the Shaw Monument. Ink on muslin banner; 59"-by-47" (p.73)

Ku Klux Klan parade float— "White Supremacy" Ink on muslin banner; 59"-by- 81" (p. 70–71)

Group Portrait in Garden. Ink on muslin banner; 71"-by-93" (p. 44–45)

Indian Baptism. Ink on muslin banner; 83"-by-103" (p. 82–83)

Adobe Church (New Mexico). Ink on muslin banner; 96"-by-129"

Civil Rights Encounter (Hosing). Ink on muslin banner; 95"-by-134" (p. 74–75)

School Kids Masking. Ink on muslin banner; 95"-by-71" (P. 55)

Indian Shaman Figure. Ink on muslin banner; 95"-by-68" (p. 54)

Hampton Alumna. Ink on muslin banner; 72"-by-59" (p. 49)

Hampton Alumnus. Ink on muslin banners; 72"-by-59" (p. 48)

Hampton: Students in the Library. Ink on muslin banner; 71"-by-86" (p. 52–53)

Hampton: Yearbook page "H". Ink on muslin banner; 95"-by-75" (p. 11)

Class in American History. Ink on muslin banner; 72"-by-90" (p. 40–41)

Weems and Buffalo Jump. Ink on muslin banner; 83"-by-76" (gate 1)

Hampton: A Class in Drafting. Ink on muslin banner; 83"-by-76" (p. 12–13)

Sappho by Dupré. Ink on muslin banner; 119"-by-175" (p. 14–15)

Hampton Graduate at Home. Ink on muslin banner; 83"-by-101" (p. 18–19)

Old Folks at Home. Ink on muslin banner; 84"-by-97" (p. 20–21)

Armstrong and Family. Ink on canvas; 103"-by-120"-by-1" (gate 4–5)

Indians—After. Ink on canvas; 72"-by-97"-by-1" (gate 6)

Indians—Before. Ink on canvas; 72"-by-97"by-1" (gate 3)

Bugle Boys. Ink on canvas; 72"-by-39"-by-1" (gate 4–5)

WHO   WHAT

NOTES FROM ESSAYS

NOTES TO PATTERSON

1. "Carrie Mae Weems, Artist," Alpert Awards, Visual Arts, 1996

2. Jacquelynn Baas, *Carrie Mae Weems: Ritual & Revolution, MATRIX/Berkeley 176* (Berkeley, Calif.: University of California Berkeley Art Museum/Pacific Film Archive, 1998), unpaginated.

3. Thomas W. Collins, Jr., interview in *Projects 52* (New York: Museum of Modern Art, 1996), unpaginated.

4. For a thorough analysis of Weems's co-dependency of image and voice, see Susan Fisher Sterling, "Signifying—Photographs and Texts in the Work of Carrie Mae Weems," in Andrea Kirsh and Susan Fisher Sterling, *Carrie Mae Weems* (Washington, D.C.: National Museum of Women in the Arts, 1994 rev. ed.), pp. 19–36.

5. Baas, unpaginated. For further background on Weems's early career and work—"Family Pictures and Stories" and the "S.E. San Diego" series—see Andrea Kirsh, "Carrie Mae Weems: Issues in Black, White and Color" in Kirsh and Sterling, pp. 9–13.

6. Kirsh and Sterling, p. 13.

7. Ibid., p. 25. For Weems the stage was the only place African Americans were allowed a legitimate public place and an acknowledgement of a positive public persona.

8. Patricia C. Johnson, "Balance at the Table," *Houston Chronicle* (April 8, 1996). See also Dana Friis-Hansen, *From Carrie's Kitchen Table and Beyond* (Houston: Contemporary Arts Museum, 1996). The artist herself has pointed out that at the time she and several contemporaries—Laurie Simmons, Cindy Sherman, Sherrie Levine, Lorna Simpson—were composing images using the conceit and context of the stage or cinematic set to posit a series of questions steeped in issues of female identity, sexuality, and responsibility. "I was trying to respond to a number of issues: woman's subjectivity, woman's capacity to revel in her own body, and woman's construction of herself and her own image" (Telephone conversation with Dana Friis-Hansen, February 6, 1996, as quoted in Friis-Hansen, p. 6; see also the interview with Weems in this volume).

9. Thomas Piché, Jr. and Thelma Golden, *Carrie Mae Weems: Recent Work, 1992–1998* (New York: George Braziller Publisher, in association with the Everson Museum of Art, Syracuse, N.Y., 1998), p. 11.

10. Ibid. In 1989 Weems said, "Let me simply say that my primary concern in art, as in politics, is with the status and place of Afro-Americans in our country" (Mel Rosenthal, "Commentary," *Nueva Luz 2* [1989]: p. 32). When asked in 1998 if she were still in agreement with that statement, the artist replied: "The thing I'm most interested at this moment is the complexity of the human experience and relationships, be they African American or otherwise. When I first started making photographs, I was very aware that there were very few pictures of African Americans and that they always stood for themselves. My sense was that the images of white people could speak about universal concerns. I wanted to use images of blacks in the same way, so that representations of blacks and materials associated with blacks could stand for more than themselves and for more than a problem, that they could speak about the human condition. But I've come to realize that the way blacks are represented in our culture makes it almost impossible to get that point across. So, now I'm asking the questions in a different way. Notions of black representation are still very important to me, and will always be a concern. In fact, it is now absolutely my assumption that people of color do speak to something bigger than themselves. I assume that that is just fine, whether writers and critics get it or not— it's not my problem. If they don't get it then my work is misunderstood and racialized" (Piché and Golden, p. 12).

11. Ibid., p. 11. See also Houston A. Baker, Jr., "Islands of Identity: Inside the Pictures of Carrie Mae Weems" in *In These Islands: South Carolina, Georgia* (Tuscaloosa, Ala.: Sarah Moody Gallery of Art, University of Alabama, 1994), p. 17. For an in-depth analysis of "And 22 Million Very Tired and

Above and opposite: "Who What When Where," 1998

Very Angry People," see Kirsh and Sterling, pp. 29-32; see also Carrie Mae Weems, "And 22 Million Very Tired and Very Angry People" (San Francisco: Walter/McBean Gallery, San Francisco Art Institute, 1992).

12. Friis-Hansen, p. 11.

13. Mary Jane Jacob, introduction in *Carrie Mae Weems* (Philadelphia, Pa.: The Fabric Workshop/ Museum, 1996), pp. 14 and 25; for a discussion of Weems's use of wall-paper designed to complement the exhibition, see p. 13. The artist has often pointed to the parallels that exist between this work (and its inherent theme) and "The Kitchen Table Series" and "Africa Series" pho-tographs—the overarching issues founded in the relationships between men and women, and the challenges women must engage in the face of this dynamic (Telephone conver-sation with Weems, June 7, 2000).

14. Annette B. Weiner and Jane Schneider, eds., *Cloth and Human Experience* (Washington, D.C.: Smithsonian Institution Press, 1989), p. 2.

15. Mary Jane Jacob, in exhibition brochure accompanying the presentation of *Carrie Mae Weems: Ritual & Revolution* in "Diaspora" at DAK'ART 98, the Galerie Nationale d'Art, Dakar, Senegal; organized by the Fabric Workshop/Museum, Philadelphia.

16. Baas, unpaginated.

17. Ernest Larsen, "Between Worlds," *Art in America* (May 1999): p. 128.

18. Ibid.

19. Weems's banners for this project were produced in Berlin, Germany, and Täby, Sweden, by Big Image Systems, Inc.

20. Paraphrased from Weems's talk to Associate Professor Shanti Singham's junior seminar in history ("Is History Eurocentric?") at Williams College, April 27, 2000.

21. Weems has discussed the complicated nature of the five-part musical composition accompanying *The Jefferson Suites*—the incorpor-ation of classical string music, a trumpet set, chanting, the duet of

Weems's and colleague Ulysses Jenkins's voices, and an original modern arrangement by Newton—linking science and music, sound and rhythm (Telephone conver-sation with Weems, June 7, 2000).

22. Karen Sinsheimer, *The Jefferson Suites* (Santa Barbara, Calif.: Santa Barbara Museum of Art, 1999), unpaginated.

23. Quoted in Meredith Tromble, "Carrie Mae Weems: DNA and Difference," *Limn* 5 (February 2000): p. 14.

24. Lindsay Rust, "The Thirteenth Floor," *The Independent* (December 18, 1999).

25. Jeanne Zeidler, introduction in Mary Lou Hultgren and Paulette Fairbanks Molin, *To Lead and to Serve* (Virginia Beach, Va.: Virginia Foundation for the Humanities and Public Policy with Hampton University, 1989), p. 6.

26. Johnston was not the only photographer to turn a lens on the Hampton Institute. The works of William Larrabee, Frederic D. Gleason, Leigh Richmond Miner, F.

Holland Day, Frances Chickering Briggs, James Van Der Zee, and the many members of the Hampton Institute's own Kiquotan Kamera Klub all testify to a healthy and varied tradition of photography on the Hampton campus. Nonethe-less, Johnston's images, undoubtedly because of their greater number and international recognition, have proved the most provocative over the last hundred years.

27. Henry Louis Gates, Jr., "The Face and Voice of Blackness," in Guy C. McElroy, *Facing History: The Black Image in American Art*, ed. Christopher C. French (San Francisco: Bedford Arts in association with the Corcoran Gallery of Art, Washington, D.C., 1990), pp. xxix-xlv.

28. Constance W. Glenn, in her essay in this book, refers to the writings of historian Laura Wexler on this theme.

29. The artist has often remarked upon the tensions she sees existing between morality and necessity, principle and power; such dualities she sees embodied in Thomas Jefferson and manifested in his

policies and premises for his version of democracy. She cites his strategies with regard to the Native American—despite his respect for the Indian and his consideration of native peoples as the equals of white men, he clearly understood and acted upon his belief that America would have to be built at their expense (Telephone conversation with Weems, June 7, 2000; see also the interview with Weems in this volume).

30. Sarah Mandle, "Weems' Exhibit Opens at Williams," *The Williams Record* (March 7, 2000): p. 10.

31. Linda Carmen, "New WCMA Exhibition Combines Great Contemporary and Historical Photographs," *The Advocate* (March 8, 2000): pp. 1, 13.

32. Linda Carmen, "Visiting Artist at Williams Talks about Her Work," *The Advocate* (March 22, 2000): p. 3.

33. Quoted from talk to Williams College Museum of Art Museum Associates (a docent group), March 15, 2000.

34. bell hooks, *Art on My Mind*, pp. 68–69.

35. Ibid., p. 70.

36. See bell hooks, "Diasporic Landscapes of Longing" in *Carrie Mae Weems* (Philadelphia, Pa.; The Fabric Workshop/Museum, 1996), pp. 29–39; also bell hooks, *Art on My Mind*; and Horace Brockington, "Re/Positioning and Hierarchy: Carrie Mae Weems, 1992–1998," *NY Arts* (December 1998): p. 19.

37. Piché and Golden, p. 13.

38. In her "Sea Islands Series," Weems appropriated and manipulated (enlarged and tinted) daguerreotypes taken in 1850 by J. T. Zealy from the collection of The Peabody Museum at Harvard University—another instance of the artist's prior work with a "pedigreed institution."

39. Piché and Golden, p. 30.

40. David Bonetti, "Visual History of Africa America," *San Francisco Examiner* (May 19, 1995): p. C3.

41. Quoted from talk to Williams College Museum of Art Museum Associates, March 15, 2000.

42. The configuration of the museum's Class of 1935 Gallery precluded the display of three of the twenty-four images designed for *The Hampton Project*: banners depicting cotton picking, a detail of Saint-Gaudens's Shaw Memorial, and the Ku Klux Klan float, "White Supremacy."

43. Of course, we can study the banners individually, but collectively, they possess greater synergy, becoming signifiers as an encyclopedic whole.

44. Barbara Michaels, "New Light on F. Holland Day's Photographs of African Americans," in *History of Photography*, vol. 18, no. 4 (Winter 1994): pp. 334–347. Saint-Gaudens was approached about a possible commission in 1881 by the Shaw Memorial Committee, an organization formed just after the Civil War by Joshua Smith, a former servant to the Shaw family and a former fugitive slave who had established himself as a successful entrepreneur in the post-war era.

45. These five pieces were originally intended to hang together with Armstrong in the center, flanked by the Native Americans; these in turn braced by the band members. Constrained by the logistics of the gallery, the brass band duo was eventually installed on the opposite wall. The implied distance between the first and second images of the Native Americans selected by Weems reveals the erasure of indigenous culture, the imposition of nineteenth-century American (white) mores, and the dramatic degree to which "the Savage" might be tamed through education and vocational training (Janet Catherine Berlo, *Plains Indian Drawings, 1865–1935: Pages from a Visual History* [New York: Harry N. Abrams, Inc. in association with

The American Federation of Arts and The Drawing Center, 1996], p. 44). Armstrong was all too aware of the propagandist potential of these images of "wild barbarous things" and was eager to "work that photograph business well" (Letters from Armstrong to Richard Henry Pratt, August 26 and September 2, 1878, Pratt Papers, Yale University). The general envisioned the now famous "before" and "after" photographs (by William Larrabee) of new arrivals at Hampton as a publicity stunt to increase revenue (Donal F. Lindsay, *Indians at Hampton Institute, 1877–1923* [Urbana and Chicago: University of Illinois Press, 1995], p. 25).

46. These very four images were part of Weems's "And 22 Million Very Tired and Very Angry People" (1991). At that time the captions accompanying the works read: "An Information System," "Some Theory," "A Precise Moment in Time," and "A Hot Spot in a Corrupt World." (Piché, p. 23).

47. W. E. B. Du Bois, *The Souls of Black Folks* (Chicago: A. C. McLurg and Co., 1903).

48. Berlo, p. 18.

49. Du Bois, chapter 1, pp. 3–4. "…the Negro is…born with a veil, and gifted with second-sight in this American world—a world which yields him no true self-conscious-ness, but only lets him see himself through the revelation of the other world. It is a peculiar sensation, this double consciousness, this sense of always looking at one's self through the eyes of others, of measuring one's soul by the tape of a Negro; two souls, two thoughts, two un-reconciled strivings; two warring ideals in one dark body, whose dogged strength alone keeps it from being torn asunder."

50. For more on Hampton's camera club see Mary Lou Hultgren, "The Hampton Camera Club" in Richard J. Powell and Jock Reynolds, *To Conserve a Legacy: American Art from Historically Black Colleges and Universities* (Andover, Mass.:

Addison Gallery of Art and the Studio Museum in Harlem, 1999), pp. 159–162; for more on Dunbar and the Kiquotan Kamera Klub see Nancy B. McGhee, "Portraits in Black: Illustrated Poems of Paul Lawrence Dunbar," in Keith L Schall, ed., *Stony the Road: Chapters in the History of Hampton Institute* (Charlottesville, University Press of Virginia, 1977), pp. 63–103.

51. It should not be overlooked that the two images of Hampton seniors were certainly devised to portray subjects as they would have wished to be seen—proud and privileged in the accomplishment of a Hampton education; and indeed, the pictures are happier alternatives to a photographic legacy of slavery. Weems' aim is to grieve with those (students) whose lives may have been diminished by a (Hampton) experience, as well as to honor and celebrate those who prospered from such an education.

52. Alvin Josephy, Jr., *500 Nations* (New York: Knopf Publishers, Inc., 1994), p. 437.

53. Berlo, p. 10.

54. Quoted from audio narrative of *The Hampton Project*, 2000, at the Williams venue.

55. Du Bois, chapter 14, p. 6.

56. Ibid., chapter 14, p. 16.

57. As of this writing Weems has editioned three additional images of this banner, but reproduced in a sepia tone with red letters and on canvas.

58. Larsen, p. 128.

59. In contrast to the narrative voices in *Ritual & Revolution* and in *The Hampton Project*, the voice in *The Jefferson Suites* is more remini-scent of a prosecuting attorney or grand adjudicator, citing evidence in support of the case at hand.

60. Quoted in interview with Katherine Fogg and Denise Ramzy, Williams College, April–May,

2000. Piché cites the relevancy of Henry Louis Gates, Jr.'s examination of African American texts in his book *The Signifying Monkey* (New York: Oxford University Press, 1988) with regard to Weems's work and briefly discusses the traditions of nineteenth-century (slave) narratives as they find their contemporary counterpart in the writings of Zora Neale Hurston (1903–1960). Weems avows great indebtedness to Hurston, attributing the discovery of her "voice" to the novelist, folklorist, and anthropologist (Piché and Golden, p. 15).

61. Wendy Liberatore, "Hampton Project," *Albany Daily Gazette* (March 24, 2000): pp. D1, 5.

62. I wish to thank Deborah Willis-Kennedy for sharing her thoughts, in a discussion on April 28, 2000, on the similarities between the Weems exhibition at WCMA and Willis-Kennedy's exhibition for the Anacostia Museum and Center for African American History and Culture, Smithsonian Institution, Washington, D.C, "Reflections in Black: A History of Black Photographers, 1840 to the Present"; see also Vicki Goldberg, "When Asserting a Self-image is Self-defense." *The New York Times* (April 9, 2000): pp. AR 39–40.

63. Sterling A. Brown (1901-1989) was a noted African American critic, author, and poet.

NOTES TO RUDOLPH

1. To Clarissa Chapman Armstrong, July 18, 1862, quoted in Edith Armstrong Talbot, *Samuel Chapman Armstrong: A Biographical Study* (New York: Doubleday, Page and Co., 1904), p. 66.

2. "Religion at Williams . . . found its apotheosis . . . in a haystack to which five Williams undergraduates retired from a nearby grove in the summer of 1806, seeking shelter for their prayers and conversations from a sudden thunderstorm. Under this haystack was born the impulse which inspired the great adventure of American foreign missions." The event was memorialized in 1867 by the erection of the Haystack Monument in the area designated Mission Park, where the 1806 prayer meeting had taken place. Frederick Rudolph, *Mark Hopkins and the Log; Williams College, 1836-1872* (New Haven: Yale University Press, 1956), pp. 14, 204.

3. John H. Denison, *Hampton's Founder and His Ideals* (Hampton, Virginia: Hampton Institute Press, 1903), p. 5.

4. To Clarissa Armstrong, December 14, 1860, quoted in Talbot, pp. 45–46.

5. To Clarissa Armstrong, April 20, 1861, quoted in Ibid., p. 53.

6. To Ellen Armstrong, February 17, 1891, Samuel Chapman Armstrong Collection, Williams College Archives and Special Collections.

7. To Clarissa Armstrong, September 1861, quoted in Talbot, p. 58.

8. To Clarissa Armstrong, March 30, 1861, quoted in Ibid., p. 51.

9. Denison, p. 5.

10. Talbot, p. 60.

11. Ibid., p. 50.

12. Quoted in Suzanne Catherine Carson, "Samuel Chapman Armstrong: Missionary to the South" (Ph.D. diss., Johns Hopkins University, 1952), p. 83.

13. To O. O. Howard, June 18, 1885, quoted in Ibid., p. 126.

14. Quoted in Howard V. Young, Jr., "James A. Garfield and Hampton Institute," in Keith L. Schall, ed., *Stony the Road: Chapters in the History of Hampton Institute* (Charlottesville: University Press of Virginia, 1977), pp. 36, 39.

15. In an 1874 letter to Williams College class of 1862, quoted in Carson, p. 211.

16. Robert Francis Engs, *Educating the Disfranchised and Disinherited: Samuel Chapman Armstrong and Hampton Institute, 1839–1893* (Knoxville: University of Tennessee Press, 1999), pp. 139–140.

17. Booker T. Washington, *Up From Slavery: An Autobiography* (Cambridge: Houghton Mifflin, 1900), p. 55.

18. To Archibald Hopkins, June 16, 1868, quoted in Carson, p. 170.

19. Quoted in Engs, p. 143.

NOTES TO GLENN

1. Lincoln Kirstein, ed., *The Hampton Album* (New York: Museum of Modern Art, 1966), p. 5.

2. The largest number of the photographs in the album were by Johnston, save a few anonymous works illustrating Negro and Indian life in contrast to the life of the Hampton graduate.

3. Pete Daniel and Raymond Smock, *A Talent for Detail: The Photographs of Miss Frances Benjamin Johnston, 1889–1910* (New York: Harmony Books, 1974), p. 34.

4. *Life*, (April 25, 1949), pp. 14-16.

5. Kirstein, p. 11.

6. Jeannene M. Przyblyski, "American Visions at the Paris Exposition, 1900: Another Look at Frances Benjamin Johnston's Hampton Photographs," *Art Journal* (Fall 1988), p. 68. This very informative study is recommended for further exploration of the Hampton assignment.

7. James Guimond, *American Photography and the American Dream* (Chapel Hill: University of North Carolina Press, 1991), p. 31.

8. Laura Wexler, "Black and White and Color: American Photographs at the Turn of the Century," *Prospects*, vol. 8 (Winter 1988), pp. 375, 383.

9. Daniel and Smock, p. 32.

10. Constance W. Glenn and Leland Rice, *Frances Benjamin Johnston: Women of Class and Station* (Long Beach: California State University Art Museum and Galleries, 1979), Appendix A.

11. Ibid., pp. 90–91.

12. Ibid., pp. 61, 79, 87.

13. Guimond, p. 24.

NOTES TO WILLIS-KENNEDY

1. Richard J. Powell and Jock Reynolds, *To Conserve a Legacy: American Art from Historically Black Colleges and Universities* (Andover, Mass.: Addison Gallery of Art and the Studio Museum in Harlem, 1999), p. 103.

2. Glenn Jordan and Chris Weedon, *Cultural Politics: Class, Gender, Race and the Postmodern World* (Oxford: Blackwell, 1955) p. 251.

3. Ann Douglas, *Terrible Honesty: Mongrel Manhattan in the 1920s* (New York: Noonday Press Farrar, Straus and Giroux, 1995), p. 98.

4. Albert Boime, *The Art of Exclusion: Representing Blacks in the Nineteenth Century* (Washington, D.C.: Smithsonian Press, 1990), p. 42.

5. Cary D. Wintz, *Black Culture and the Harlem Renaissance* (Houston: Rice University Press, 1988), p. 31.

6. Ibid.

7. Judith Fryer Davidov, *Women's Camera Work: Self/Body/Other in American Visual Culture* (Raleigh, N.C.: Duke University Press, 1998), p. 159.

8. Ibid., p. 166.

CREDITS AND ACKNOWLEDGMENTS

I dedicate this book to my brother John Weems.
—Carrie Mae Weems

Many people have shared generously their time, knowledge, and enthusiasm in the production of *The Hampton Project*. At the heart of the effort, the staff of the Williams College Museum of Art undertook and sustained the many rigors and innumerable tasks related to the organization of this book, the exhibition, the symposium, and the national tour. But for their teamwork, the project would have never come to fruition. My sincere thanks go to Director Linda Shearer for having conceived of the exhibition and assured its development; Associate Director Marion Goethals, ever-stalwart, for overseeing its daily progress and its financial support; Education Director Barbara Robertson along with Artists-in-Residence Karen Shepherd and Cecelia Hirsch and the Museum Associates, who carried out a tri-state educational outreach program and daily interpreted Weems's work to the public; Curators Deborah Rothschild, Nancy Mowll Mathews, and Ian Berry for their insights and counsel; the Preparation Department—Hideyo Okamura, Pat Holden, and Greg Smith—who worked with the artist to install the exhibition as well as assisted with the photographic documentation; Public Relations Assistant Kay Kamiyama, who managed the exhibition graphics and assured the project's public presence in Williamstown and beyond; Mellon Curatorial Assistant Stefanie Spray Jandl, who proposed Ms. Weems's candidacy as Sterling A. Brown, Class of 1922, Visiting Professor and arranged the curricular links on campus; Registrar Diane Hart Agee and Registrarial Assistant Rachel Tassone for their care of the artist's work in Williamstown and attention to the logistics of the tour; Director of Membership Judy Raab and Membership Coordinator Ann Greenwood for their efforts culminating in a most memorable symposium on race and education; Secretaries Amy Tatro, Sheila Mason, Laura Champagne, and Accounts Manager Dorothy Lewis for their always cheerful and precise secretarial support; Museum Security for their diligent oversight of the exhibition and the safety of the artist's work; and student interns Elyse Gonzales, Tess Mann, Olivia

Vitale, and Margaret Adler who, over the last four years, have stepped into the fray with energy and ability.

Though not museum staff, but "family" nonetheless, photographer Arthur Evans triumphed over adversity in his unflagging pursuit of the perfect image of Ms. Weems's diaphanous banners. In the pictures that so beautifully illustrate this volume, he captured the ethereal qualities of the installation and the individual pieces of the fabric suites.

I want to express my appreciation to Constance W. Glenn, Deborah Willis-Kennedy, Frederick Rudolph, and Jeanne Zeidler for their enlightening essays that give historical perspective to this undertaking. Also, Katherine Fogg and Denise Ramzy, both Williams College class of 2000, coordinated a series of interviews with Ms. Weems during the spring semester. Excerpts from several transcribed texts are their important contribution to this book, informing the artist's intent and accentuating her voice within the parameters of *The Hampton Project*.

John Marcy, Director, Northampton Photographic Arts, and D. James Dee, Director, The Soho Photographer, Inc., graciously lent their hands in the printing of many photographs for the catalogue; Pamela Vander Zwan has been a constant source of help with myriad details of the artist's work and career; designer Beth Carlisle has worked tirelessly to bring images from *The Hampton Project* into the public arena in the form of invitations, brochures, and posters.

The assistance of a number of friends and colleagues on campus helped guarantee the success of our exhibition and publication efforts: Steven B. Gerrard, Associate Dean of the Faculty and Associate Professor of Philosophy; Alex W. Willingham, Director of the Multicultural Center and Professor of Political Science; Associate Professor of Political Science Mark T. Reinhardt; Sylvia Kennick-Brown, College Archivist and Special Collections Librarian, and Linda Hall, Senior Circulation Assistant; Multimedia Instructional Technician Bruce Wheat; Wendy Hopkins, Director, and Paula Moore Tabor, Associate Director, Alumni Relations; Thomas Bleezarde, Editor of the *Williams Alumni Review*;

The Shape of Things, detail from triptych from "Africa Series," 1993

Sandra L. Burton, Assistant Professor of Physical Education and Coordinator of Dance; and the members of the Hampton Project Planning Committee.

For essential funding of the project, in addition to those agencies mentioned in the director's introduction, I would like to give special recognition to Gary Burger at the John S. and James L. Knight Foundation, Tomas Ybarra-Frausto at the Rockefeller Foundation, and Clay and Garret Kirk, Williams College class of 1963.

I am indebted to Museum of Modern Art Curator of Photography Peter Galassi, Associate Curator M. Darsie Alexander, and Curator of Photography, Emeritus, John Szarkowski for invaluable information and ultimately for the loan of vintage Johnston photographs to the exhibition along with entrée to MoMA's files and archives for research; the dedicated staff members of the Hampton University Museum and Archives, who for four years have provided us and Ms. Weems with access to their own Johnston holdings and many additional records about Hampton's history; Director Doug Munson and Associate Director Toddy Munson at Chicago Albumen Works in Housatonic, Massachusetts, for their production of contemporary platinum prints from Johnston's originals and for their expert advice regarding the photographic medium; Director Tom Branchick, Senior Paper Conservator Leslie Paisley, and the staff of the Williamstown Art Conservation Center for their help in developing and installing the exhibition; Big Image Systems in Täby, Sweden for their assistance to Ms. Weems in digital reproduction of images onto muslin; and certainly Jeffrey Hoone, Director of Light Works, Syracuse, New York, for proving a most gallant go-between with the artist as the occasion demanded.

Ms. Weems's representatives at P. P.O.W. in New York, Penny "Rave" Pilkington and Wendy Olsoff, who, along with their staff, have been extremely generous with their time and resources. It has been a pleasure working with them. Editor Phyllis Thompson Reid, Editorial Assistant Meredith Coeyman, and Designer Michelle Dunn Marsh at Aperture Foundation have energetically supported this book, often proceeding on blind faith and fueled by the opportunity to work with a woman photographer; the association has been both fruitful and extremely enjoyable. I thank my colleague Curator Wendy Watson at Mount Holyoke for our initial introduction.

Susan Dillmann, whom I think a paragon of enthusiasm and dogged initiative, has assisted me throughout the preparation of this work; I am grateful for her participation and for her expertise as Editorial Consultant on this publication.

The key figure in this endeavor, of course, has been the artist herself. Carrie Mae Weems availed us of her work, her time, her energy, her patience, and her good humor. We hope this volume does credit to her art practice, and we thank her unremittingly for her support of our Hampton Project.

—VIVIAN PATTERSON
Williamstown, June 2000

EXHIBITION SCHEDULE:
Carrie Mae Weems: The Hampton Project

Williams College Museum of Art, Williamstown, MA, March 4—October 22, 2000

International Center of Photography, New York, NY, January 27—April 15, 2001

The High Museum of Art, Folk Art and Photography Galleries, Atlanta, GA, June 2—September 6, 2001

The University Museum, California State Long Beach, January 29—April 27, 2002

The Nelson-Atkins Museum of Art, Kansas City, MI, October 20, 2001—January 6, 2002

The Hood Museum, Dartmouth College, Hanover, NH, September 14—December 1, 2002

Carrie Mae Weems, *The Hampton Project*, 2000, digital photographs printed with water-soluble pigmented inks on muslin and canvas, courtesy of the artist and P.P.O.W., New York; page 25 in collaboration with The Fabric Workshop/Museum; page 26 courtesy Peabody Museum; page 34 *Bush String Quartet*, courtesy the Corbis Bettman Archives; Frances B. Johnston photographs on page 64, 65 (left), courtesy The Museum of Modern Art, New York, and on page 65 (right), courtesy Hampton University Archives; page 59 and center gatefold courtesy Williams College Archives and Special Collections; pages 8 courtesy California State University, Long Beach; page 60 courtesy Hampton University Archives; page 63 courtesy Library of Congress.

Carrie Mae Weems and Aperture Foundation are grateful for the kind permission of the following to use archival images as source material for the banners and canvasses, pages: 11–13, 18–21, 40–41, 44–45, 48–49, 52–53, and gatefold except center image, courtesy Hampton University Archives. Page 81 *Weems With Buffalo Jump* background image courtesy the Estate of David Wojnarowicz and P.P.O.W.; page 31 (left), courtesy Ullstein Bilderdienst; page 31 (right), courtesy the Photo Archive Group; page 51 unidentified image, probably from a negative made ca. 1895-1900 for a stereograph series on the South, from the Underwood & Underwood Glass Stereograph Collection, Archives Center, National Museum of American History; page 54 courtesy Princeton Collection of Western Americana; page 82-83 Daniel McArthur performing a baptism on a Shivwitz Indian, courtesy the Historical Department of the Church of Jesus Christ of Latter-Day Saints; page 70-71 courtesy the V. A. McFeely Collection, Fitz-Symms Photography; page 74-75 copyright © Charles Moore, Black Star; center gatefold image courtesy Williams College Archives and Special Collections.

Library of Congress
Catalog Card Number: 00-103933
Hardcover ISBN: 0-89381-913-1

Photo Credits: Arthur Evans: pages 2–5, 8,14, 16–19, 36–41, 44–45, 47–51, 62–65, 73–74, image in photo insert between pages 16 and 17, gatefold images, 82–83. D. James Dee: pages 15, 42–43, 67–68, 69–70, 87. Will Brown: page 27.

Design by Michelle Dunn Marsh

Printed and bound by Tien Wah Press (PTE.) LTD., Singapore.

The Staff at Aperture for *Carrie Mae Weems: The Hampton Project* is
Michael E. Hoffman, Executive Director
Phyllis Thompson Reid, Editor
Stevan A. Baron, V.P., Production
Lisa A. Farmer, Production Director
Olga Gourko, Design Associate
Meredith Coeyman, Editorial Assistant
Eileen Connor, Editorial Work-Scholar
Heather McGinn, Production Work-Scholar

Aperture Foundation publishes a periodical, books, and portfolios of fine photography and presents world-class exhibitions to communicate with serious photographers and creative people everywhere. A complete catalog is available upon request.

Aperture Book Center and Customer Service: 20 East 23rd Street, New York, New York 10010. Phone: (212) 598-4205. Fax: (212) 598-4015. Toll-free: (800) 929-2323. E-mail: customerservice@aperture.org

Aperture Foundation, including bookstore and Burden Gallery: 20 East 23rd Street, New York, New York 10010. Phone: (212) 505-5555, ext. 300. Fax: (212) 979-7759. E-mail: info@aperture.org

Visit Aperture's website: www.aperture.org

Aperture Foundation books are distributed internationally through:
CANADA: General/Irwin Publishing Co., Ltd., 325 Humber College Blvd., Etobicoke, Ontario, M9W 7C3. Fax: (416) 213-1917. UNITED KINGDOM, SCANDINAVIA, AND CONTINENTAL EUROPE: Robert Hale, Ltd., Clerkenwell House, 45-47 Clerkenwell Green, London, United Kingdom, EC1R OHT. Fax: (44) 171-490-4958. NETHERLANDS, BELGIUM, LUXEMBURG: Nilsson & Lamm, BV, Pampuslaan 212-214, P.O. Box 195, 1382 JS Weesp, Netherlands. Fax: (31) 29-441-5054. AUSTRALIA: Tower Books Pty. Ltd., Unit 9/19 Rodborough Road, Frenchs Forest, Sydney, New South Wales, Australia. Fax: (61) 2-9975-5599. NEW ZEALAND: Southern Publishers Group, 22 Burleigh Street, Grafton, Auckland, New Zealand. Fax: (64) 9-309-6170. INDIA: TBI Publishers, 46, Housing Project, South Extension Part-I, New Delhi 110049, India. Fax: (91) 11-461-0576.

For international magazine subscription orders to the periodical *Aperture*, contact Aperture International Subscription Service, P.O. Box 14, Harold Hill, Romford, RM3 8EQ, United Kingdom. One year: $50.00. Price subject to change. Fax: (44) 1-708-372-046.

To subscribe to the periodical *Aperture* in the U.S.A. write Aperture, P.O. Box 3000, Denville, New Jersey 07834. Toll-free: (800) 783-4903. One year: $40.00. Two years: $66.00.

FIRST EDITION

10 9 8 7 6 5 4 3 2 1